To

With wishes of peace.

DIVALDO FRANCO
BY THE SPIRIT
JOANNA DE ÂNGELIS

A SOWING
OF LOVE

Translated by
Claudia de Almeida

Authorized edition by
Centro Espírita Caminho da Redenção. Salvador (BA) – Brazil

Miami
1st ed. 2022

ISBN 978-1-953672-31-5

Original title in Portuguese:
Messe de Amor
(Brazil, 2021)

Translated by: Claudia de Almeida
Revised by: Ily Reis
Edited by: Luciano de Castilho Urpia
Layout and cover design by: Rones Lima – instagram.com/bookebooks_designer

Edition of
LEAL PUBLISHER
8425 Biscayne Blvd. Ste. 104
Miami, FL 33138, USA
www.lealpublisher.com
(305) 306-6447

Authorized edition by Centro Espírita Caminho da Redenção – Salvador (BA) – Brazil

INTERNATIONAL DATA FOR CATALOGING IN PUBLICATION (ICP)

F895   Franco, Divaldo (1927)

    A Sowing of Love / By Spirit Author Joanna de Ângelis [psychographed by] Divaldo Pereira Franco ; translated by Claudia Dealmeida ; revised by Ily Reis ; Miami (FL), USA Leal Publisher 2022.

    188 p.; 21cm

    Original title: Messe de Amor

    ISBN: 978-1-953672-31-5

    1. Spiritism 2. Psychography. 3. Moral Reflections. Title I. Franco, Divaldo Pereira, 1927 – II. Title.

CDD 133.93

CONTENTS

BIOGRAPHY

Sister Joanna Angelica de Jesus was born on December 11, 1761, in the city of Salvador, State of Bahia, Brazil. At the age of 21, she entered the Lapa Convent, becoming a nun of the Reformed Religious Order of Our Lady of Conception. Due to her numerous merits, she was made an abbess in 1815.

During the Brazilian struggle for independence from Portugal, she stoically defended her Convent. To the Portuguese soldier who cowardly stabbed her with his bayonet on February 20, 1822, she said the words that translate the greatness of her resolute spirit: *this entryway is guarded by my chest, and you will only get in over the body of a dead woman.*

From the spirit world, under the pseudonym Joanna de Ângelis, she has been significantly contributing to the elevation of the human spirit as an Emissary of the Lord in the work of humankind's re-Christianization.

Introduction

Allan Kardec, the blessed Apostle of the *Third Revelation*, wrote in the first chapter of *The Gospel According to Spiritism*[1], under Items 6 and 7:

"... Spiritism is the Third Revelation of God's Law, but it is not personified in any particular individual; rather, it is the product of a teaching given not by one person but by the Spirits –the *voices of heaven*– at all points of the earth and through a countless multitude of intermediaries. It is a sort of collective entity entailing a group of beings from the spirit world, each one coming to bring to humans the tribute of its knowledge in order to enable them to know about that world and the fate that awaits them in it.

"In the same way that Christ said, 'I have not come to destroy the Law but to fulfill it,' Spiritism says, 'I have not come to destroy the Christian Law but to fulfill it.' It teaches nothing contrary to what Christ taught, but develops, completes and explains in clear terms for everybody what He stated only in allegorical form. Spiritism has come to fulfill at the foretold time what Christ announced and to prepare the fulfillment of future things. It is therefore the work of Christ, who Himself is presiding –as He also announced– over the regeneration that is occurring, and who is preparing the reign of the Kingdom of God on earth."

For that reason, Spiritism is a sowing of love, waiting to become an abundant harvest in the human heart.

---

1 1ˢᵗ Ed. International Spiritist Council. – Tr.

Considering that some of the pages in this book have already been disseminated by Spiritist and secular publications alike, we have revised and summarized them to better integrate them into the whole, always ensuring that they preserve their original spirit.

We do not presume to present a new path for struggling Spirits –as is our case– immersed in the evolutionary battle.

We just want to contribute, however minimally, to the efforts of the Blessed Workers from the *Greater World*[2] who have embraced the difficult task of implementing the expansion of the Kingdom of God in the human heart, at a time when the grateful and happy Spiritist family commemorates the first Hundred Years[3] of the publication of *The Gospel According to Spiritism* in Paris, France.

Bringing back Jesus Christ' Good News, Spiritism magnifies love, inviting human beings to a fraternal crusade of redemption for a better and happier world.

We realize, however, the limited value of our effort, considering the extensive Spiritist and evangelical bibliography already existing on the subject.

As the Sowing of the Lord is incommensurably rich with light, we felt encouraged to present these pages –dictated over a period of more than ten years– with no literary or exegetical pretense.

They add nothing to the cultural patrimony of many.

It is a modest Christian-Spiritist glossary that seeks to awaken sleeping consciences and Spirits distracted in relation to everyday events –which often surprise us, threatening our inner peace.

Knowing that, if the molecules contained in an apparently insignificant drop of water were to be transformed into grains of sand they would span the length around the Equator, the message of Jesus –which Spiritism broadens and disseminates– if exemplified by edifying actions would cover the entire Earth with love and light.

---

2 Reference to the spirit world. – Tr.
3 *The Gospel According to Spiritism* was first published in 1864, and *A Sowing of Love* was first published in 1964. – Tr.

We would like to conclude this introduction by quoting the eminent *Codifier*[4] of Spiritism:

"... *Spiritism has come at the stated time to fulfill Christ's promise: the Spirit of Truth presides over its establishment; it calls humans to observe the law and teaches all things by enabling them to understand what Christ said only in parables. Christ stated, 'Let those hear who have ears to hear'. Spiritism has come to open eyes and ears because it speaks without figures or allegories. It lifts the veil intentionally left over certain mysteries. It has come, finally, to bring supreme consolation to the disinherited of the earth and all those who suffer, attributing a just cause and useful purpose to all pain.*"[5]

Hoping to have achieved our goal despite our flaws and imperfections, we acknowledge in Spiritism the loyal Messenger, the interpreter of the Spirits, and the announcer of the New Era, while we entreat Jesus, the Master par excellence, to bestow His blessings on all of us.

Salvador, February 1, 1964
JOANNA DE ÂNGELIS

---

4 Allan Kardec (1804-1869), pen name of French educator Hippolyte *Léon Denizard* Rivail. – Tr.

5 *The Gospel According to Spiritism*, Ch. 6, Item 4 (1st Ed., International Spiritist Council). – Spirit Auth.

1
LONELINESS AND JESUS

When the adversities of the journey scar your soul, hitching you to the black chariot of loneliness, remember the Master and how He was terribly abandoned at the time of the Crucifixion.

Where were all the old friends, the satiated multitudes, the hearts He had helped?

He began His ministry –to which He would completely give Himself over– in the joyful occasion of The Wedding at Cana and He ended it on the Cross, forgotten by the countless people He had constantly helped amid their loud racket.

The Master was always surrounded by people…

He preached in the beautiful surroundings of cities and villages, at the beach, by the lake, on mountains, in filled Synagogues, and in bustling town squares.

He received all those who asked for His help.

His entire apostolate of love was about ennoblement.

To the disdained and humiliated woman, He offered the most beautiful expressions of His Message.

He consoled and enlightened the tormented woman from Samaria.

He removed the spirit obsessed[6] woman from Magdala from her cushions of velvet and silk.

He invited Martha to reflect on matters of the Spirit.

He received the Canaanite woman and restored balance to her spirit obsessed daughter.

---

6 Spirit obsession: The domination that certain spirits acquire over certain individuals. Allan Kardec, *The Mediums' Book*, Ch. XXIII, #237 (International Spiritist Council). – Tr.

Hannah, Peter's mother-in-law, received His healing *passes*[7].

He restored the health of the poor, Syrophoenician woman who was hemorrhaging.

To the widow of Nain, He gave back her son who was thought to be dead.

Joanna, wife of Chuza, received His invitation to partake immortal life.

He awoke Jairus' daughter from the clutches of catalepsy.

And, beyond them, He extended His love to all hearts.

Lepers and healthy people alike lived with Him.

Illustrious men and beggars received His affection.

The man from Gadara –who was under attack by spirit obsessors– regained his peace of mind. Jesus also healed the Centurion's servant.

He enlightened Saul, the wealthy prince by the Sanhedrin, during a fraternal dialogue, and He gave the gift of sight to the blind and vagrant man of the streets of Jericho.

He honored the lavish palace of Zacchaeus, and ate in the humble boats of impoverished fishermen.

He revealed the Good News to the learned men of Jerusalem who listened to Him in awe, and, at the last hour, He taught two thieves who were crucified alongside Him how to enter through the narrow door to achieve spiritual liberation.

He bestowed movement upon the paralyzed legs of Nathaniel –who was lowered through a hole in the ceiling– and revealed to the Baptist's disciples the signs by which they could verify that He was the One they had been waiting for.

Thousands of souls received peace and health from His hands.

Demons surrendered to His voice.

The sea followed His orders.

The wind obeyed His command.

Diseases disappeared under His touch.

Angels carried out His will...

And yet, in His hour of anguish, He drank from the bitter cup alone.

---

7 Passes: A transfusion of energy that alter the cellular field... In magnetic assistance, emission and reception are entwined, helping needy patients so that they can help themselves." (Andre Luiz, *In the Realms of Mediumship*, Ch. 17 (International Spiritist Council). – Tr.

The female heart at the foot of the Cross offered Him only longing and tearful affliction.

He experienced agony, mockery, and humiliation in extreme abandonment.

Not one voice spoke in His defense before the High Courts.

The people who had received so much love, who had broken into a delirious applause only the day before by the city gates, had now forgotten all about Him.

Still, putting His complete trust in God, He defeated the world with its deceptive propositions, and, even after death, He reemerged in all His glory, returning to His sowing of love to everyone's gladness.

Remember Him.

Alone in the world, but with God by His side.

In your most difficult hour, your friends and the objects of your affection cannot stay with you; they must move forward. Life is also waiting for them.

Be patient.

Do not love them any less because of it. They need your understanding and your love.

Grow, so that you may help them to grow as well.

And even if death snatches your flesh, you will be reborn after the ashes of the sepulcher, in a radiant dawn, to continue your work alongside the very people who abandoned you.

In your loneliness, however, Jesus is always with you.

2
IN HONOR OF AN IDEAL

You are being summoned to build a better world, and that is how you will gain access to the world that you truly long for.

Rejoice, be enthusiastic, and do not stop.

Do not give in to malicious criticism and protect your ears from unfair accusations.

Do not succumb to gratuitous enemies. Only idle people have time to put up a pointless defense.

Look at the life of heroes and pioneers. They were all misunderstood and disrespected.

The laughter of a handful of individuals –entrenched in skepticism and foolish ignorance– many times exploded in a noisy cackle to humiliate them. Their mordancy, however, was defeated by the ideal that they defended and that future generations confirmed.

Aristarchus of Samos proposed the Heliocentric System five centuries before Christ. Galileo, however, not too long ago was forced to deny that fact.

When Eratosthenes of Cyrene calculated the circumference of the earth with crude and rudimentary instruments, he stated that it measured 39.690 kilometers –for which he was seen as insane. Now, modern science, with the help of very sophisticated equipment, measures the same circumference and states that it measures 40.075 kilometers...

Hipparchus of Nicaea said that the solar year lasted 365 days and 6 hours minus 4 minutes and 48 seconds. He was ridiculed. And, recently, his mistake was found: his calculations were off by 6 minutes.

Preaching the doctrine of universal love, Jesus was crucified alone and relegated to mockery for centuries. And yet, the humanity of the future would be tasked with rediscovering Him for the sake of its own happiness in the times to come.

Go into action.

Respect time by using it properly.

Appreciate small, positive things.

Develop your qualities for service.

And do not stop on account of the pessimism exuded by the defeatist, or the false superiority of those who triumph in the realm of illusion.

Your faith speaks about the excellence of Christian duty. You cannot be afraid.

You will always run into accusers along the way and the difficulties will be many.

Make the decision to triumph and do not stop.

Seemingly credible voices will accuse you.

They will ridicule your character.

They will criticize your behavior.

Pay no attention to them.

Although adorned and finely dressed in expensive materials – exhibiting a tenuous social veneer– they still are what they are.

Many dogs wear precious stones on their collars, but they continue to be dogs.

Though he slept in a palace and ate out of a silver platter, *Incitatus* was still a horse.

Artifices do not change reality.

High heels do not add any real height to a short person.

A stall built of gold and silver cannot change the quality of the feed for the animals.

Based on all the above, align yourself with the good, even at the price of blood, sweat, and tears...

Disseminate the truth, encourage order, engage in noble service, preach duty, forgive ignorance, love always, and insist on the principles of pure Christianity.

There is a lot of land to clear, and there is a lot of work to be done for the sake of the future.

Smile and forgive, putting forth your absolute best, and proceed.

And if you are not able to see your dreams come true because you must leave the physical plane, you will watch from a better Sphere how other resolute individuals continue your work, feeling grateful for your anonymous heroism.

3
DOMINATION

M any individuals dominate in the world…
Owners of large tracts of land that change hands.
Owners of herds that die.
Holders of assets that disappear.
People with great fortunes that vanish.
Commanders of men that perish.
Rulers of consciences that find freedom.
Academics that succumb to pride and madness.
Domineering and dominated people everywhere.
Bosses who answer to other bosses.
Proprietors who are but temporary keepers.
Masters who are slaves to their vices.
There is only one type of genuine domination: the power over ourselves.

Renewed by the light of the Gospel, examine the scope of your dominion, and feel the force that comes from the Heavens. Can you control your anger and continue to help someone who does not understand? Can you suffer injustices for the Christian Cause that you espouse and defend? Can you persevere when others abandon the great ideal? Can you maintain a moral conduct amid terrible temptations born of the invigilance of many? Can you practice renunciation continuously in order to ascend? Can you forgive no matter what, and continue working in the vineyard despite ongoing challenges?

If you can persevere when others give up, insisting on fraternal ways for the good of all, and if you can control and manage your anger, laziness, fear, greed, wounded pride, and remain committed and loyal to your faith, then you have acquired the power that comes from the Heavens and that no one can take away. A power that will make you a genuine servant of Christ on the way to redemption.

4
DISCIPLINE

The divine order spreads throughout the whole Creation:

The little seedling rising up in search of the solar energy that sustains it.

The sun submissively orbiting around the center of the galaxy that serves as its cradle;

The worm, crawling within its limited resources;

The river waters tamed by dams generating hydroelectric power to advance progress.

When disrespect upsets the order of things, one can expect upheaval and chaos.

Order is the twin sister of discipline, which maintains production and fosters progress.

In your case, reincarnation is a school of enlightenment, but also a disciplinary prison where you acquire the values to help you ascend and find freedom.

Your noise upsets the neighbors, who watch you with displeasure.

Your irritations affects your friends, who get angry in turn.

Your transgressions of the law harm society, which will restrict your freedom of action.

On the same token, your struggle to become better gets noticed.

Your smiles spread joy.

Your true friendship enriches the lives of your fellow human beings.

The hope you spread around comforts many hearts.

You must realize, however, that giving and receiving require discipline.

You will not receive undue concessions from Life's Abundance to the detriment of other Spirits.

Because you wish to change the solar trajectory to enjoy a greater amount of light and heat, the sun will not change its course to suit you. It will remain obedient to the gigantic orbit that disciplines it and keeps it in place.

You tame the lower animals to use them for household tasks. However, the dog that defends your home is the same dog that attacks an intruder. Its instinct has been disciplined.

The wood used in building a bed is the sibling of the paddle used to punish. The use of the wood has been disciplined.

The water that quenches thirst comes from the same spring as the water that can be used to poison. Its purpose has been disciplined.

The hands that applaud are the same hands that can hurt. An indiscipline in their use, because the body submits to the will.

Consider that the useful household container was made from muddy clay.

The cake owes its shape to a humble sheet of aluminum.

The electric light, which brightens the darkness, results from a colossal force that was being lost.

In order to fulfill its specific purpose, each thing must adapt to a certain form of discipline.

We understand discipline as the set of duties born from an imposed or consented order.

Even the Truth, to be beneficial to human beings, must be administered in small doses.

Sunlight, which makes life on earth possible, is filtered and measured out to tend to the needs foreseen by the Celestial Father, without causing harm.

Thus, people's happiness depends on the discipline they impose on themselves.

Education of the will.

Upright action.

Impulse control.

There must be order in our activities and duties, maintaining a high level of respect and moderation in the exercise of our natural functions.

Remember Jesus when He said:

"I did not come to abolish the Law but to fulfill it."

5
HOWEVER IMPERFECT

There are those who, under the pretext of imperfection, silence any edifying words on their lips, thereby imprisoning the consoling message.

There are those who, justifying their own imperfection, paralyze their arms in the ministry of moral health, stopping the work that saves.

There are those who use their own imperfection to cultivate laziness and spread uselessness.

There are those who use their own imperfection to do nothing for their fellow human beings, claiming to be stranded in the same place of unhappiness and affliction…

Fill yourself with love, however, abandoning your iniquity to help other iniquitous people.

Love is a tree that must be planted in order to produce.

The Spiritist Doctrine teaches that no one is reborn on the earth to continue to cultivate the toxic behaviors of the past or to continue to make the same mistakes…

Reincarnation is a blessing.

Goodness is a shining light.

Before taking the plunge into the flesh, we all begged for the blessing of pain and suffering to better understand the pain and suffering of others.

No one can rightly speak about a subject they know nothing about, or have no first-hand experience.

And for that reason, you will often teach resignation while riddled with anguish; you will talk about a disease while your own soul is ill; you will console while needing to be consoled; you will show the need for understanding while experiencing incomprehension; you will preach justice while crushed by other people's impiety; you will nurse your brothers' and sisters' wounds, while the core of your being has multiple open sores.

While others wait to achieve personal sublimation in order to help, you must start helping right now.

We all deal with issues that pain our souls, but the work we do for others is the medication that will soothe our own agony.

While you teach the very peace that your heart does not have, and you show others how to overcome temptation while you are in its very grip, your Spirit improves and learns about the dignity of duty, which slowly becomes a ladder for your spiritual ascension.

And even if you are crucified by your own imperfection, keep advancing without fear. Remember that the Master who, despite His own suffering, abandonment, and apparent defeat on the Cross of shame and impiety, still found the strength to elevate His soul to the Merciful Father out of concern for the wounds in the human heart of all times, and tenderly pleaded:

"Forgive them Father! For they know not what they do."

Do likewise. Forgive, love, and help always.

6
A DIFFICULT FORM
OF CHARITY

You give your coat to wrap someone's frail body, pouring into your heart the serenity that comes from your gesture of charity toward the needy.

You offer bread and clean water generously, and experience the inner joy born from the sublime charity towards the hungry and the thirsty.

You give money, and feel the emotion that results from aiding those in need.

You spread compassion, and harmonize your conscience with the charity extended to the morally afflicted.

You offer medication, and renew yourself through the blessing of helping the sick.

You kindly provide shelter, filling your soul with the peace derived from your act of charity toward the homeless.

You forgive an offense, providing the warmth of faith to the wounded Spirit by forgetting the evil that rises from the heart of the wicked and deceived.

And by practicing charity in several ways, as taught by the evangelical message, you think you are conjugating the verb "to love."

However, you can still do more.

If you wish to fully integrate into the Christian spirit of charity, go further.

There are other Spirits around you waiting for invisible hands capable of helping.

You probably do not know them, see them, or hear them, and, perhaps, they are not in your circle... But they are there.

You will find out about them through the Spiritist Revolution that has brought them to light. They are the tormented Spirits beyond the grave, our discarnate suffering brothers and sisters.

Some became your enemies *yesterday,* and now bring affliction to your physical existence; others sleep, hypnotized; some ignore the *country* they now inhabit; others live in the tormenting memories of the past; some gather in groups and experience their shared anguishes; others cry because they are *hungry, thirsty, adrift, cold, and sick...*

They are all sufferers snatched from their physical life by death.

They all need us...

Since you know Spiritism and its spark shines bright within your soul, pray for them, love them, and think about them, sending them positive, helping vibrations when the opportunity arises within the Spiritist cells in which you militate during your physical journey. Receive them, and offer them the healing Spiritist words that encourage, console, awaken, guide, and heal...

Offer them your psychical *antennae* and let them communicate through your mediumship, so that they may benefit from your charitable efforts.

You will suffer their influence as you help them.

You will intimately share their agony and affliction.

They will not always disconnect from you right away.

Some will linger by your side, waiting, and you will feel them...

You will experience intimate and silent conflicts under their influence...

Have no fear of them, though.

Do not rebel.

Entrust them to Jesus, the Divine Medium, considering that they need someone to love and help them from the earth.

Think how happy you would be if you could find someone willing to offer their physio-psychical resources for your liberation. So, do what you would have them do to you. And from now on, you can start practicing that difficult and neglected kind of charity that the world does not see, and your friends do not reward with premature praise or unnecessary adulation. And remain certain that Jesus –who has loved us for millennia– never tires to bestow His ineffable mercy and love, even in the abyss of inferiority in which we still linger...

7
THE PRACTICE OF PRAYER

When affliction besieges your work and batters your heart, or incites negative thinking, remember the simple act of prayer that is within everyone's reach.

Like a sublime balm, it does not only heal the open wounds in your heart, but it also vitalizes your most cherished dreams badly impacted by the dark cloud of desperation, restoring your hope and peace.

Like a good angel, prayer improvises resources for salvation to put out the flames of crime at the start, so that serenity may return to guide the conscience.

It not only guarantees happiness and harmony in the home, but it bestows beauty on all your actions. It offers new motivation and courage for the complete success of the experiences thanks to which you improve yourself while you are in the world.

It consoles, heals, and brings light to your troubled thoughts by restoring your calm and clarity, so that you may free yourself from the shackles fastened to your feet, keeping you in the realm of endless anguish.

A sowing of inexhaustible blessings, prayer is the sanctuary of the family, the sustenance of the children, and the resiliency of the parents.

A messenger of the Celestial Father, it is the interpreter of your aspirations, and intercedes for your wishes with the Higher Spirits.

Flowing faithfully from the heart, prayer calms our passions, purifies our sentiments, establishes guidelines, moderates our needs, strengthens our faith, and elevates our standard of service. And in relation to our learning, it harmonizes our dignity, our respect, and our spiritual health, improving the scope of even our smallest tasks as we help those who suffer.

Espousing prayer, our minutes become hours rich in sublime experiences, making life more noble and dignified.

On the earth, Christians are like fertile oases in a desert of sentiments.

Requested by everyone and closely monitored, they are like fruit trees that the hungry seek out while reserving themselves the right to pelt and harm them at will.

Thus, endure silently gratuitous persecution and the invisible dagger of evil, wrapping them in humble and noble prayer where all adversaries of the light fade away, defeated by the mercy of the Heavens.

And whenever possible, cultivate prayer in your soul trustingly and devotedly. Working tirelessly, make it your blessed guide for every day and every hour, and it will guarantee the victory of the good in the journey of your life.

8
COMPLAINING

Rid yourself without delay from the habit of complaining, and extinguish the flares of impulsivity that drives you to commit hasty acts that push you away from your duties to life.

Complaining can be compared to a dangerous and lethal acid.

It leads to evil speaking, which in turn encourages slander and foments disrespect.

We all carry wrongs committed in past lives, which reemerge in the present as thorny afflictions to rectify mistakes, correct imbalances, and reinforce our fortitude.

For that reason, all difficulties can be considered as a favor from the Divine Law, for they give us the chance to simplify and rebalance our soul.

What seems like an unfair trial is but an indispensable atonement.

The obstacle that hinders our advance and prevents us from succeeding on the earth –for the moment at least– should be accepted as a gift from life or a celestial favor.

So do not make your own problems worse by complaining.

While we complain and spread our bitterness, we amplify the negative aspect of what is but an opportunity to make amends, creating discouragement and sadness.

All souls long for friends who are willing to listen as a testimony of solidarity.

However, while complaining flows through our lips –like the inner rebellion that it is– we waste valuable time we could spend to improve ourselves.

Complainers get used to lamentation and get entangled in their own net.

They are always bitter.

It is always nighttime in their Spirit.

While they are locked up in the dungeon of wounded pride, precious minutes pass and leave them empty-handed.

In the language of duty, complaining can be translated as rebellion and interpreted as insubordination.

Trying to avoid making amends –through painful experiences– is not worth much because it complicates the problem, which will return with its intact load of pain and affliction asking for reparation. What we fail to do now, will return either today or tomorrow demanding resolution.

Insulted and arrested amid sarcasms and shoving, the Lord descended from the Mount of Olives surrounded by the forces of temporal power, who were brandishing clubs and torches ready to perform the supreme mockery. He was taken to jail while remaining in absolute silence, in which He sought communion with the Father in order to find in the Divine Source the strength for the final victory.

Wrap your bitterness in the fabric of silence, just like He did.

Keep your commitment with suffering within your soul with a robust Spirit and a heart full of faith and tolerance.

The gentle fountain defeats the muddy bottom to quench the thirst of those begging for fresh water.

Overcome your difficulties wherever they might be, and rise from the river of mud in which you linger.

Do not abuse your friendships with your complaints.

You would not dare to offer those who seek you out a plate full of ashes or a glass filled with vinegar.

Complaining breeds negativity and encourages laziness.

Get your Spirit used to the discipline that rectifies so that your actions may be spontaneous.

Honor your friends with the hope that your trusting smile inspires.

Offer kind words to those who surround you with affection. And, when you come across good listeners –strong and courageous– remember that they could be facing their own inner struggles, and are also looking for someone to offer them support to heal the open wounds they bear in their hearts.

9
SERVING AMID TEARS

You yearn to ascend in the task of the Sowing of Light, but are not willing to pay the price asked of those who wish to embrace the blessing of service.

You wonder how it is possible for many brothers and sisters to maintain an attitude of dignity, while handling diverse responsibilities in their assistance to those who suffer.

In your case, every attempt to serve has been characterized by failure, pushing you back.

It could come in the way of misunderstandings that rise unexpectedly, and turn into tormenting afflictions.

It could be difficulties that appear inexplicably, preventing your march and becoming obstacles difficult to remove.

It could be conflicts that erupt violently and turn in to a blaze, devouring the joy.

It could be aggravations that are continuously repeated, causing the bread of hope to grow stale.

It could be unwarranted persecutions that trigger panic and agony in your mind, frightening and battering you.

It could be friends who frequently desert you, abandoning important responsibilities that turn into crushing burdens.

And now you feel your hands calloused, your feet swollen, sweat running down your face, your heart pained …

In the meantime, the others, those who continue to smile, are also experiencing great upheavals while remaining steady at their posts.

And, while they smile, their hearts are frequently hurting with a pain that does not let up.

While they lend their assistance, with their minds often burning, their own restlessness mingles with the affliction of others.

Nonetheless, they transform their pain into strength and carry on, without complaining, certain that deserting their duty would only complicate the situation they are trying to flee.

Do not lament or wish for the kind of unproductive peace that lingers in idleness.

The anonymous base of a monument does not complain about its lower position. However, without it, the work of art would have no support to allow it to be seen and admired.

Pain, silent and anonymous, is fundamental to the success of any endeavor.

May the satisfaction to serve be an honor to you.

Thus, learn to transform the tears with which duty is testing you into smiles of encouragement for those who are less strong, certain that we are all in the struggle, suffering to learn and serving amid tears. Connect your thoughts to the Lord who, to this day, without complaining, has not found in our souls a safe place for peace and proper rest.

10
KEEP AT IT!

When Henry Ford explained to the great captains of the electrical industry the details of the gasoline-powered engine he built in 1896, Thomas Edison exclaimed "*keep at it!*"

And, focusing his mind on the marvelous idea, he revolutionized *the horse-less carts,* opening horizons to a new era.

No idea per se is either so perfect that it does not need improving, or so imperfect than it cannot be adjusted.

The coin that buys someone's medication to treat an illness has also passed through the hands of criminals.

Often times, a good idea begins as something rudimentary and unrefined, but after some valuable modifications, it becomes a blessing in the lives of many.

People who change their minds frequently almost never accomplish anything of value.

To succeed at any endeavor, it is indispensable to *keep at it.*

Without perseverance which helps us improve, hasty endeavors almost always fail and leave us feeling bitter and aggravated.

Every idea has something good about it when we can implement it to benefit someone.

A burning flame is a vehicle for purification, just as rotting garbage is a source of fertility.

Do not try to evolve along the lines of Christianity by improvising…

For twenty centuries, the idea of Christ has been shaking the earth without having totally entered into the human heart.

However, persuasive and kind, He continues to offer the necessary material for the transformation of the character of humankind according to the guidelines of His doctrine of love.

If you have been touched by the invitation to participate in True Life, keep at the idea of renewing yourself inwardly, and carry out the tireless battle for the good of all by removing the inner obstacles hindering your ascension.

Fire persists and devours otherwise impenetrable forests.

Light insists and develops the embryo of life.

A small brook persists and creates a mighty river.

A grain of wheat persists until it becomes bread.

A chiseled stone reemerges in a different shape.

A drained swamp is reborn with a different appearance.

An irrigated desert reappears modified.

Persist in implementing your higher ideas and change the pernicious ones that pay a visit to your mind.

Raise your thoughts to Jesus Christ –the Sublime Idealist – and let Him inspire you, impressing in your core the incoercible force of the Good in the form of life and joy for yourself.

11
ENVY

It is easy to cry with those who cry, offering our tears as an expression of empathy and emotion.

Where there is pain, the soul wants to help, offering the blessed treasure of solidarity.

To the sick, we offer medication, and to the hungry, very few people would deny a piece of bread.

In the face of pain, even hardened hearts shed tears and extend their hands, trying to help.

It is natural to come down to help when one enjoys a higher position.

There is, however, a different and forgotten kind of charity, behind whose closed door you could help souls that got lost in harrowing abysses, trapped in cruel depths.

We could see it as the joy that results from sharing other people's happiness.

To be in the lowlands of scarcity and bless the abundance of those in the highlands.

To experience the joy and the satisfaction of our friend's successes without wanting or asking for anything.

To share the happiness that smiles at our friends and neighbors from the silence and the affliction of our own anguish.

But frequently, however, we let our spite and envy distillate their venom in our soul.

If the victory belongs to an old friend, we shy away, saying *he has changed!*

If he seeks us out trying to help us, we feign humility and say that *everything is fine!*

And all the while we mutter, we hurt, we strike, we slander...

In the inner recesses of our being, our invigilance sets up traps for our repressed anger, and if the person falls for whatever reason, we say that *it was only a matter of time. Pride is always punished!* Inside we keep a deceitful smile of satisfaction while on the outside we try to help, not in the good sense of the word, but from a place of superiority because we are the ones providing the assistance…

Spiritists, my brothers and sisters, you know that there are many tears wetting fine linens and many wounds hidden beneath expensive clothes that cannot be seen.

Greed is a merciless snake. Do not feed it so that it does not poison you.

But also help those who seem to be happy by praying for them.

Stay away from envy, just as you would keep your distance from contamination by a terrible disease.

Steer clear of gossip.

Drown pernicious spite in prayer.

The simple prick of a needle can cause a horrible infection, just like a drop of venom can be death's messenger.

Use kind words. Flowers are identified by the scent they give off.

When your night is dark and your heart is heavy, remember how the sky has millions of resplendent stars above the heavy storm clouds, and that even the thistle that is disdained in silent abandonment, blooms at night and fills the air with fragrance.

Remember the Carpenter from Galilee, who reached out to Simon –the rich tax collector– blessed his wealth, and had a memorable dinner at his elegant palace despite the fact that, at the climax of the gathering, a poor spirit obsessed woman seeking His help received the sap of eternal life –as a breath of hope for all of us– in the words, *all your sins have been forgiven, for you have loved much.* Continue to be happy wherever you might be while you deal with difficult problems that money, power, or other concessions –all of them divine loans– could solve, as you watch them pour into the hands of other people in large amounts.

12
THE GREAT GOOD

D o not forget the efficacy of prayer along the path of the great
good.
When we are in the service of higher ideals, we frequently run
into storms at every step.

In multiple ways, conjugated forces lie in waiting ready to assault
our inner peace by way of brutal and well-directed blows.

The sky of decisive Christians is not always clear when they are in
the service of Jesus.

For the time being, the earth cannot understand, and friends
cannot help.

Some people have the right disposition to cooperate, but they look
at everything through the wrong lens with a mixture of detrimental
pessimism and unproductive anxiety.

If they remain faithful to the task and proceed confidently, they are
seen as self-sufficient and prideful and, therefore, in great danger...

If they listen to other people's advice, they are seen as indecisive
and lacking courage...

If they solve the problems as they arise, without consulting with
their fellow workers, they are seen as arrogant and excessive...

If they give themselves wholeheartedly to the point of sacrifice,
they are seen as fanatical and insane...

If they find in caution the antidote for failure, they are seen as not
having faith...

If they offer the other cheek to their aggressors, they are seen as
lacking character...

If they prevent the situation from being repeated, they are seen as false Christians…

Among fellow workers, there rarely is fraternity without incomprehension, suspicion, demands, or acrimony.

So do not give evil more importance than it has, which is actually very little.

We are children of the Light…

Let's put our trust in the Light of the Heavens…

Are clouds of slander hovering over your work? Walk toward the sun of the truth.

Is the plague of intrigue attacking the plantation of faith? Apply the insecticide of courage and keep marching toward the truth.

Are suspicions and lies besieging your field of work? Increase your faith in time and continue to move toward the truth.

Are different ailments afflicting you? Keep working and moving toward the truth.

The work of the good for the good of all has a high price tag.

Do not deny your plantation the contribution of your own sweat.

Do not deprive the tender seedling the moisture of your tears.

Remember the Divine Master –a tireless postulant of the Eternal Truth– crucified by crafty intrigues, but Alive and Immortal after the shadows of the sepulcher, returning to His accusers to extend to them the glory of the triumphant Good News.

13
SUFFERING AND AFFLICTION

They are intertwined in every situation.

Suffering caused by the evocation of a passionate and fleeting love, and the affliction of those who, not having loved, wish to be needlessly enslaved.

Suffering caused by the wish to persecute at will, and the affliction of those who, being persecuted, do not have the opportunity to persecute in turn.

Suffering caused by a pain that yearns to be sheltered in the heart, and the affliction felt for not being able to do all we want, further complicating our situation.

Suffering caused by an unchecked ambition that corrupted our character, and the affliction resulting from the fact that, having had so much, we were unable to enjoy as much as we thought.

Suffering caused by our rebellion for not having found happiness as delineated in our plans, and affliction for having had happiness within our reach only to realize how much darkness and tears hide under the cloak of that illusory kind of happiness.

Suffering caused by the realization that, though we have much, we actually have nothing, and affliction for having nothing and discover how much we could have.

Suffering on the cross of imbalance, and the affliction of imbalance on the cross of repairing duties.

The suffering of those struggling to rehabilitate, and the affliction of those in error lacking the strength for rehabilitation.

The suffering that crushes, and the affliction in search of ways to crush others.

Nonetheless, suffering is a means of purification, and affliction a vehicle of suffering for those who, having found the liberating truth, opt, for their moral rehabilitation, the blessed path where the Spirit finds itself, after the pointless battles on the road travelled by those who are distracted and unhappy.

You have learned with Jesus that suffering for internal rehabilitation spells liberation, and affliction to seek self-renewal spells ascension.

So, strive to eliminate the evil still existing within you. Pay the price in terms of suffering and the affliction of your conscience. Remember that, before the clear and luminous morning of the glorious Resurrection of the Master, there were the darkness of treason and the infamy of cruelty as valuable lessons. So, before the resplendent morning of triumphant immortality, you will face the night of silence and testimony, which will lead you, however, to the radiant celebration of light and permanent freedom.

14
THE SIGN OF CHRIST

Do not be ashamed of your limitations as you embrace service in the name of Christian love.

Remain on the path of the good, bringing happiness to the people, even if you yourself are thirsty while distributing water. A contribution born of sweat and tears is a sign of authenticity.

Many fellow workers will point to your mistakes, trying to inhibit the words that you place at the service of the Good News. Keep at it, anyway! Because you know that, when the time comes and the Lord pleases, He will seal your lips leaving you silent.

Many will remind you of the moral flaws that dishearten you, as you help the morally bankrupt rehabilitate themselves. Persevere in your work, certain that the Lord will paralyze your arms whenever He feels is the right time.

You will come across those who are familiar with your imperfections, and cannot admit that you have become a vanguard for the sublime ideal that you advocate. Be sure, however, that when the Lord desires, He has the resources to remove you from the scene.

So, remain walking on the narrow path of faith and working on behalf of charity without boundaries.

Acknowledge your own flaws, but do not dwell upon them.

Only parasitic plants feed off trees without reservation.

Jesus is Life and the Christian Doctrine involves activity.

Go forward!

Work for the good and for your own well-being.

Do not lend your ears to the venomous wickedness of others. All accusers are sick people caught in the grip of grave diseases.

And if, trying to hurt your feelings, they should say that you know a doctrine by the quality of the people gathered under its banner, remember in silence the Galilean Group. It was made of thieves, impoverished people, and unhappy individuals. Judas stood out as a traitor and Peter stood out because He denied knowing Jesus, and yet both were chosen to be His friends. And it was thanks to them that the unbreakable bond of pure faith became known during three centuries of martyrdom, as they fertilized the soil with the bloody sacrifice of their own lives. Thanks to them, you know the Divine Friend today…

If the people who believe to be healthy only knew about the vile diseases that ravage their bodies, they would collapse in horror.

We discover cancer once it becomes detectable. But who could accurately say when normal cells first became cancer cells?

To regard the earth as a Large Hospital because thousands of people are hospitalized in it would be too pessimistic, considering that the planet is a blessed school for souls.

While many wait to achieve their own purification first before they start helping others, many morally infirm individuals die in misery.

If doctors refused to take care of their patients because they are not feeling too well themselves, the practice of medicine would be compromised.

Do not be disheartened by the poison of gratuitous accusers.

Those who stand by the side of the road can only see a part of it. And because of that fact, they do not deserve your anguish.

Let them be, weak and sick, wherever they choose to be.

Go forward! Even while being conscious of your inner limitations, remember that no thirsty person ever inquired about the moral qualities of someone handing them a glass of water.

Thus, no one will ask who you are or where you come from either. They will ask what you have to give in Jesus' name as a sign that He is with you and that you are with Him.

And connected to the Spirit of the Christ through love and charity, illuminate the night of the souls, until His Light blazes within you, setting your entire being aglow and burning away your last inequities.

15
IN REFERENCE TO MONEY

On the earth, things have the value that you assign to them. Case in point: money.

With money you buy bread, and you go after the crazy adventure of power or the crazy power of adventure.

Most people live to make money and they accumulate it at the price of slander, persecution, and personal unhappiness…

They are the notoriously unhappy millionaires who cannot find peace.

Others, however, suffer the terrible consequences of the all-out battles that they fight to build wealth.

They are the unhappy ones that suffer because they do not have it. However, those with money could be happy if they consented to the joy of bringing happiness to the unhappy. And happy are those who believe to be unhappy because they do not have money, and yet they are blessed because they do not face the dangers of being enslaved by assets that perish with the body and are the very cause of its destruction.

When money is put in its proper place as an instrument of exchange, individuals find the enlightened path to inner happiness, far away from the capital torments into which the oblivious jump headlong.

Money per se is neither a blessing nor a curse. It is an instrument of exchange. To have it or not have it is neither a reason for happiness nor for unhappiness. What matters is the person's state of mind.

If many are slaves to *what they possess*, many are the submissive servants of *what they do not have*. So, the money that could be a friend turns into an enemy, forcing people to live for it.

Money simply cannot ever buy true happiness: a spontaneous smile, the love that is born of a pure sentiment, or the peace that results from a genuine friendship…

Though it can acquire many things on the earth, money is more a factor of dissatisfaction than peace.

And that is why, perhaps, the popular saying goes, *the happy man had no shirt…*

Raise your mind above the everyday struggle, tapping into the divine thought disseminated all over our Father's House. And you will hear the clear message of happiness speaking silently through *a thousand voices*: love and serve; forgive and move on; sow the good in every way possible. And, always trusting, you will find within yourself the incorruptible treasure of inner harmony, which nothing can buy or destroy. And you will return to your customary routine, joyful and free of the anguish of attachment to money, following the One who, being the Lord of the world became a servant to all, as a Model of Perfection.

16
OPINIONS

Respect your friends' opinions and analyze what they are saying judiciously. However, do not be held back by other people's points of view, which originate in the conventional wisdom of the masses.

Human respect and hypocrisy lend them a value and a strength that cannot touch you.

Because you help everyone indiscriminately, they will call you a fool.

Because you believe in God without fear, they will see you as naïve.

Because you love much and with abnegation, they will call you weak.

Because you practice mercy in the name of the Heavens, they will label you a fool.

Because you exercise prudence for yourself and others, they will call you disingenuous.

Because you teach and live the truth, they will reject you for being fanatical.

Serve and persevere, even if the mocking masses turn against your work.

Smile and move on, even when you hear the jeering all around you.

You will not stop being prudent because they ignore your poise.

You will not be less wise because they do not recognize your wisdom.

Even though those voices do not consider your respect for family and the Law, and your submission to God by loving your neighbor, examine their verbal instructions. They are the ones lecturing and writing about legal matters, duty, justice, work, morals, faith, culture, and science.

Their leaders exhibit their academic credentials and establish the rules of conduct for long periods of time, immortalizing their names on large plaques. Their worship of vanity, however, does not allow them to practice what they preach.

The wordiness with which they embellish what is essentially simple, kills the spirit and discredits within them the legitimacy of what they affirm.

Remain confident!

Opinions are dispensable accessories. Only right action constantly put into practice will teach you the lessons relating to the duties you have before the Heavenly Father.

Do not grow tired of them, and do not antagonize them.

Be neither irritated nor discouraged. All of those in service to the good have been the victims –without reason– of disdain, sarcasm, and reproach in the opinion of the people…

17

TEMPERANCE

In your Spiritist work temperance is of the essence.

Temperance that reflects, speaks, and establishes attitudes…

You will frequently experience abuse disguised as good sense and error passing for honorability, as you wait for strong voices to come and strike the lies with the tools of the truth in order to remove the mask of deception wherever it might be…

Likewise, you will hear offensive words from the mouth of infamy, deceit successfully convincing in the cobweb of illusion, and empty vanity expanding its circle…

You will easily see truth trapped in winding pathways, knowledge misapplied, and the program of legitimate human values used for the wrong purpose. However, you are not there as a judge or to pontificate in the name of the truth using severity, hastily hurting other people's feelings, persecuting, or destroying hope… Many of those who are wrong, and persist in their mistakes, are sick…

Your conduct should represent the light and the good. It should be peaceful and constructive.

The blessed task you are responsible for contains in and of itself the values that can maintain clarity in other people's hearts, and attest for the integrity of your objectives.

Not that you should condone error or applaud dishonesty. That would be to increase crime and senselessness.

Connected to the Sublime Friend through powerful bonds, walk toward Him through the sowing of love of which you are a part, certain that He is responsible for the superior task of correcting the Spirits in need who jump willingly into ghastly abysses…

As an advocate of the remarkable cause of the Heavenly Father, He knows how to apply corrective measures in the name of justice with a steady hand and a loving heart, clarifying misunderstandings, doubts, and certain notions.

So, maintain your temperance and learn to trust time, even when it seems to conspire against the ideal that is your goal.

Control your anger, which is a lethal poison that ends up killing its host.

Abandon the path of error and transform your existence into a sanctuary of honor, since, when we deceive, we only punish ourselves in a maze of excess and perversion.

Eliminate your anxiety by practicing the good because anxious persons, propelled by their impulsive nature, will be defeated as they tread along dark pathways.

Close your mouth to negative concepts, since a vessel used to contain toxic miasmas is not suitable to hold special fragrances.

Purify yourself and you will purify the entire world, following Jesus wholeheartedly and acting in His name every day of your life, with temperance and equilibrium, modeling your behavior on His.

Convinced that a sowing of love does not generate hatred, and the practice of the good cannot become one of evil, remain loyal to higher responsibilities for as long as it takes, and you will awaken –after the ashes and the mud into which your body will transform– free from mental torment and in possession of a serene heart and a mind at peace.

18
REMAIN LOYAL TO YOUR FAITH

You hear the clamoring of the insane masses…
Desperate shouting voices reach your ears…
Roaring laughter coming out of loud parties reverberate in your soul as if they meant happiness…

In the banquet of illusions, characters in the day-to-day comedy parade before your eyes…

Your teary eyes follow them as if expressing your loneliness in a world that is lost in confusion…

You would like to join them to participate in their joys and pleasures…

They seem to be so happy!

They call you and mock the fact that you keep your distance; they want you to participate in the pleasant game of sensations, and ridicule your allegiance to dignity; they appeal to your senses and rebelliously state that you have become totally repressed, that your flesh can no longer even feel anything…

They present you with insane propositions and, because you remain loyal to your duties, they mock and disrespect you. And you realize that you are maladapted to the modern world…

Spiritist faith —which disseminates the thoughts of the Christ— and profane behavior —which resonates with Mammon— are incompatible. The Christian morals of Spiritism and the malleable behavior of the citizen of the world are at opposite ends…

It is certain that you will walk alone, and many times will experience a certain anguish as if it translated your pain. But do not be afraid to suffer. Those who hesitate in the face of duty hardly ever reach their goal. You must crush all the appeals of the *old you* with the power of your resolve, so that, from the torn fibers that regenerate, the *new you* may be born. Just like through the metamorphosis of the caterpillar, a fluttering butterfly emerges ready to glide and swoop freely through the air...

Your friends will not understand. They will argue that faith has nothing to do with a person's behavior –as if they could separate cause and effect.

They will also say that you need to live like other people live. They will tell you that you should not travel down a parallel path, like a marginal person. And this is understandable. When virtue is ashamed to show itself because dishonesty gets all the applause, it is natural for someone who lives a dignified and dutiful life to be stung by fear amid so much despair. Example, however, is the light of life, and the One who is calling you preferred mockery and the renunciation of Cesar's embrace to being a guest at the palatial residence of the prefect of Israel.

Preaching the sermon of the good example, He did not triumph amid those who triumph in the world, but He outdid all of them as a champion of champions.

You can do the same. And you will, if you maintain an intimate connection with Him and remain loyal to Spiritism, which gives you plenty of resources during times of scarcity and affords you happiness when things are difficult, as you are able to discover hidden treasures of light in the folds of darkness...

You know that you return from a past many thousands of years long, scarred by grave mistakes. And by the scars that threaten to become fresh wounds again, you know that the badges of honor of a Christian are the marks of victory in a war-torn Spirit...

You must keep watch over your peace.

A lamp without oil cannot give light.

A river that does not dare to flow around obstacles does not reach the sea.

You are a growing Spirit, so even if the blows of the hammer of suffering seem strong, there is no reason to fear them.

A block of marble only becomes a statue —acquiring shape and beauty— after sustaining the sweeping strokes of the chisel.

So, let pain chisel away at your core, and a pure Spirit advancing toward the infinite will emerge from the multiple personalities that you preserve from failed reincarnations...

Stand firm in your conviction regarding immortality, and you will see that the human rings of power have no value when fingers cannot support their weight.

You will learn, my combatant friend, that the good battle will soon be over. And you will emerge luminous like a ray of sunlight that has detached from the Sun and can travel across space in total bliss, can pass through anything without suffering contamination, and can journey forever without ever extinguishing itself.

19
AFFINITIES

For the Spirits of Light to develop an affinity with you, you must mobilize the resources of the physical body, renewing concepts and attitudes in relation to its use in all your days on the earth.

Primitive emotions are more readily registered because they abound in every department of the planet.

Thus, for you to assimilate and reflect the images of spiritual life, you need to regain the original purity that your body had when you received it from the hands of the Noble Benefactors before birth.

End your complaining and sadness, and your psychical abilities will become more malleable.

Stop the reproachful language and hypocrisy that contaminate the vocal apparatus, and inspiration from the On High will flow more abundantly through your mouth.

Regain your emotional equilibrium, and subtle vibrations will envelop your body.

Discipline your nerves, and the whole system, enjoying an enviable harmony, will turn you into a perfect conduit for heavenly vibrations.

Develop good sentiments and be in communion with the beauty of eternal truths, through a pure and noble faith that will console your soul and that of many others.

And, even beyond that, the tutelary angels –sympathetic to your tireless efforts– will come to you attracted by the meaningful emanations of your lofty desires.

If, however, you do not intend to remain engaged in the lengthy battle for the light against the heavy darkness of the past –manifesting in vampirizing *thought-forms*[8]– do not expect the connection with the Pure Spirits, because the vibrational difference between you and them will hinder any undeserved attempt at establishing such a sublime bond.

We all receive divine help when we try to elevate the nature of our goals. However, we should remember that each conscience is free, and will bear the consequences of its spontaneous choices.

Free yourself right now from the yoke of perverse Entities with whom you share an affinity dating from the past. And breaking with those retentive bonds, elevate your thoughts to the higher Spheres. Commit your arms to continued work and let the idea of freedom fill you with joy, knowing full well that Jesus –who is still waiting for you– will receive you with open arms at the end of the fierce struggle.

---

8 Thought-forms: ". . . thought can be materialized, creating forms that are often of lengthy duration, depending on the persistence of the way in which they are expressed." Andre Luiz, *The Mechanics of Mediumship*, Ch. 19, "Ideoplasty" (Feb Publisher). – Tr.

20
COMPLAINTS AND EFFORT

Before complaining, make sure that you are not the very reason for your failure.

Constant complaining drives away the generosity of our friends.

Some hearts have turned into a cup of bitterness, dominated by the chronic habit of unwarranted complaining.

Masked or mordant, the unfortunate invective is always accompanied by its sad entourage in its unfortunate task.

When we learn how to overcome, we do not stop in the face of obstacles.

A water source does not complain about the muddy bottom, and a seedling does not complain about the weight of the soil that obstructs its growth.

To overcome difficulties or the influence of evil and perverse characters, the only resource we have is to strengthen our hearts with the light of love and the clarity of wisdom.

Everyone bears afflictions and problems while in the world because the earth is a blessed school where individuals struggle to learn how to break free from the millenary ghosts of crime and extreme debasement –the offspring of ignorance.

Thus, the educational process that is necessary to help us overcome evil cannot be delayed. And instead of complaining about it, we should try to elevate our ideas and sentiments.

Without a course of action meant to solidify our higher objectives, our desire for inner improvement is pointless and complaining is harmful.

We must first learn to live honorably, even if living in a physical body prevents us from seeing clearly.

Those unaccustomed to the struggle for the ascent cannot expect to rest in higher planes.

Convenience is the enemy of action.

If fierce struggles shackle your mind to a harmful past, remember that there is always time to start over and overcome.

Do not allow your indecision to characterize your quest for peace.

Do not perturb other people's peace with your unrelenting difficulties.

Make an effort and renew yourself incessantly.

Manage your anxiety with prayer; handle your bitterness with work; overcome your melancholy by lending help to others; defeat your boredom by working the soil; deal with your disappointment by continuing to work on behalf of the good; dismiss your anguish by bringing joy to others; eliminate your pain, offering your frailty to Jesus Christ...

Do not stop to examine or lament, lingering in the realm of tears and sorrow as if you had been forsaken.

Turn your eyes to the dawn, be dazzled by the light of the Sun and move with it...

When the Master seemed defeated, reviled and injured, He gave Himself over for the happiness of all —without complaint or reprisal— offering posterity the legacy of His sublime and unsurpassed example. Do likewise!

21
STAY IN THE FIGHT

L ift your dejected spirit and continue to fight.
The earth broken up by the plow produces more.
The fountain disrupted by a bucket quenches more thirsts.
A pruned tree gives more fruit.
The heart more frequently visited by pain improves more.
Do not get tired of fighting!

Reincarnation is a blessed opportunity provided by the Heavens for us to renew ourselves morally, to make things right, and to pay off our past debts.

Do not be afflicted by the urgent need for atonement.

Bless the moments of pain, which pass just like the moments of joy. Make headway in your struggle, get up when you fall, strive for the ideal, and endure suffering in order to serve. Wherever you go, you will be faced by struggle in the name of the work that elevates humankind.

True heroes are born in times of strife, and suffering is the sublime source from which true servants originate.

There are mothers who became heavenly angels during times of suffering; hearts that became sublime repositories of love; and individuals who self-renewed, becoming sentinels defending the unfortunate.

Stay in the fight!

Forget that you are tired and offer messages of consolation; stop crying and dry other people's tears with the handkerchief of your understanding; calm your restlessness and keep talking about immortality –of which your soul is saturated by the zephyrs of the spirit world– to those who know nothing about life beyond the grave...

Soft breezes will bring you blessings and speak to your ears when you quiet yourself down to pray.

Do not waste the opportunity and become dispirited when pain pays you a visit.

When you least expect it, a misunderstood angel will softly approach your physical body, and, sealing your lips with the seal of disincarnation, will unexpectedly take your soul. At that moment, you will be happy you stayed in the fight.

And, if you think that your present trials seem greater than your resilience, remember Jesus, the Crucified Angel, who despite His own suffering at Golgotha still answered the plea of the unfortunate thief, giving him hope with the possibility of entering Paradise. And be certain that, if you stay in the fight, you already are in paradise.

22
PHENOMENA AND DOCTRINE

Look for Christ alive in any school of faith to which you adhere.
What matters is not adopting a set of beliefs for the apparent advantages it can offer. What is essential is to be aware –through personal experience– of the ideals giving life to those beliefs.

In the traditional sense, a set of beliefs is simply the name of a certain religion.

But the science of it is to be in communion with the faith by actively participating in its principles.

So, it is critical to probe into the spirit of the faith to see if it is legitimate or not.

A believer is simply a passive observer.

An aware person is an active doer.

Believers act outwardly. They adopt a certain external attitude, follow formulas, are stirred by the sermons, contribute sparingly, give an account of their belief, are pleasers…

Those who are aware, however, act from the inside. They are not concerned with appearances, do not follow rituals, assign no value to hierarchies, are rarely pleasers, live fully…

At the first problem, believers complain and flee, while those who are aware suffer and fight.

Believers succeed in the world, because they are of the world. Those who are aware do not triumph in the world, because they break with superficial human conventions.

Believers succeed, receiving honors and social prominence. Acclamation gives them a veneer of false superiority and a label of saintliness.

Those who are aware seem to be defeated. They lose their interest in vain objects, triumphing over themselves and setting themselves free. No one discovers their value.

However, it is in them that the voices of the Christian Message resonate, calling out to their anxious and loyal souls.

External phenomena are fleeting.

Inner and consistent facts become a doctrine that stays.

Thus, in Spiritism, do not concentrate on the phenomenon of mediumship.

In all epochs of Humanity, the voices of the Spirits have spoken intelligibly and clearly. But there is no information that the intermediaries of these voices gave themselves over selflessly to the task of their own elevation and fraternal assistance to others.

Some fled the world and sought refuge in silence, as if they were blessed beings. They were called saints.

Others entrenched themselves in self-assigned privilege and went mad, overtaken by the seductive forces of presumption. They were known as wizards.

Only a few persevered until death, silencing the voices as their bodies were consumed by tormenting flames. They were the martyrs.

Today, some individuals who seek Spiritist practical sessions identify the Spirits, receive help, and then move on, still deluded about their final destination...

Others, irresponsible and futile, linger in research, wanting more, always more...

They believe now, but doubt later.

They are enthusiastic today, but lose interest tomorrow.

It is important, however, that you remember the application of Spiritism, and that you concern yourself with the spirit of the Doctrine.

The mediumistic phenomenon is a means, the Doctrine is an end.

The phenomenon is shapeless, the Doctrine is clarity.

The phenomenon attracts, the Doctrine guides.

The phenomenon is an instrument of the Doctrine. The Doctrine is the life of the phenomenon.

The phenomenon without the Doctrine is no more than a bunch of information without value. The Doctrine without the phenomenon, however, remains indestructible as a powerful vehicle of enlightenment and salvation.

The mediumistic phenomenon preceded the Doctrine, the Doctrine surpassed it.

Thus, in the Spiritist Doctrine look for the active Christ, and bonding with Him through the science of the Spiritist belief, proceed tirelessly in your program of self-improvement, striving for the redemption of all.

23
THE KINGDOM OF HEAVEN

With a great deal of excitement, you researched noble and moving pages containing the language of the Kingdom of Heaven.

You listened to eminent speakers addressing the excellence of the Kingdom of Heaven.

You read about missionaries that erected entire temples to house the messages from the Kingdom of Heaven.

You committed to memory ardent teachings concerning the pathway to the Kingdom of Heaven.

You meditated in ecstasy on the landscape of the Kingdom of Heaven.

In utter fascination, you dreamed about the chance to enter the Kingdom of Heaven.

And yet, you are still on the earth…

Mire and suffering everywhere.

Ignominy and crime in a deluge of hatred filled with poisons and pestilence.

Lies and treason framing human beings' minds.

And you let the bitterness crease your face, crushing your soul.

You would like to use the trampoline of faith to clear the distance from the tumultuous ocean of human affliction to the celestial highlands on one leap.

Little do you know that the authors of pages filled with beauty also suffer in the valley of shadows, thirsty for light.

Little do you know that preachers carry thorns in their hearts, and have hands scarred by hard work.

Little do you know of the tears shed by apostles during their blessed ministry.

Little do you know about the great gap between teaching and action. You do not even realize that there is a lot of heaven to be discovered in the human heart, and a lot of light hiding in the landscape of afflictions.

Heavenly heaven begins by toiling the earthly ground, just like a large tree is born from a minuscule seed.

Develop your perception and sharpen your ears.

Many propose social peace while caught in endless family feuds.

Others teach the truth through cunning expedients, as if astuteness were the best tool at the service of the ideal.

You will find missionaries busy within the churches, while souls lie neglected without spiritual guides or clothes.

Do not try to create a paradise for yourself distant from the fraternal work with marginalized communities.

And do not believe in rest that is not justified by hard work.

There is much happiness that is no more than negative idleness, just like there are many expressions that are no more than verbal poison.

The Master says, *the Kingdom of God is within you.*

Help those who suffer; watch your attitudes; spread the light of understanding; work tirelessly, observing that an abandoned plot, when worked with love and perseverance, becomes a fragrant and colorful garden.

Thus, look to the sublime realities of the Heavens, but first sublimate yourself on the earth, transforming it into a blessed garden of perennial happiness, one step away from the glory of Immortality.

24
EVEN NOW

In the noble teachings of the *New Revelation*[9] that enriches your life, Jesus continues to be the pathway, and the message of the Gospel, narrating His journey, continues to be the usual program.

Therefore, even now, there is no other alternative to deal with the different circumstances of life than that inspired by His Life.

Forgive everyone.
Follow the higher guideline without fear…
Transform thorns into flowers…
Convert vinegar into fresh water…
Watch and pray…
Love everyone…
Serve without questioning…
Assist those who persecute you…
Forgive always and proceed without resentment…
Give away your coat, even if that is all you have…
Trade the stones of affliction for the currency of light…
Turn on the light of discernment…
To faithfully follow the program that the Master Himself exemplified – that is the guideline you cannot ignore.

In any endeavor, humble tasks are also valuable.

Similarly, in Christianity you too are a valuable worker, despite your limitations.

The Master did not consider Simon's suspicions, but rather taught him, with simplicity, the unforgettable lesson of love when the sinner washed His feet with the tears of her renewed feelings.

9 A reference to Spiritism. – Tr.

Understanding Martha's justified weariness, He praised Mary's interest, thirsty for inner harmony.

So, learn how to execute the divine program whatever the circumstances.

Though nighttime can be terrifying, it also invites meditation.

Though silence can be scary, it helps us to think.

Though pain is uncomfortable, it invites reflection.

Value time, place and opportunity and do the best that you can.

It is better to reach the end of the evangelical journey alone, with your heart torn, your feet bleeding and your hands calloused, but feeling at peace, than to be surprised by disincarnation surrounded by pleasures and friends who can do nothing for you, as far as the state of your conscience as it stands at the gates of Immortality.

25
DONATIONS

Wishing to prove their own renewal, many new Christians try to show that they have changed just because they are parting with a few superfluous possessions.

They help a Christian entity by making a financial contribution, but they want to impose their will as far as the donation application.

If the entity is under construction, they disagree with the original plans and propose changes...

If the entity offers shelter to the homeless, they would like to see some changes, and, if contradicted, they antagonize the administration...

They expect subservience on the part of those who work and live there. They feel that they *own* the enterprise.

Though they are technically very kind, they are inflexible.

They believe in the *charity* they practice, but they demand submission.

They believed themselves to be high achievers, and thus expect a place of bliss they do not deserve.

Many people make donations when they join a faith. Few, however, know how to give in a way that *the left hand does not know what the right hand is doing* —as taught in the Gospel.

Indifference to money is not difficult, and we see respectable examples of this every day.

However, more important than material donations as a testimony of inner improvement are the renunciation to *points of view*, the fight against *wounded pride*, the effort to overcome rancor, the struggle to restrain personal whims...

We hear plenty of declarations of loyalty to the Christ everywhere, but few can accomplish it by fulfilling the entire gamut of indispensable responsibilities.

They ignore that an insignificant spark can create a blaze, just like any faulty electrical connection can be lethal.

When the opportunity to donate something arises, convert the small flames of pride into a blaze of discipline, guiding the force of your internal drive toward doing the Good to achieve the Christian ideal. Thus, you will slowly defeat the enemies of your inner peace while offering clothes and transitory coinage for educational purposes, growing through anonymous and selfless work on behalf of the good for all, according to Allan Kardec's statement:

"WITHOUT CHARITY THERE IS NO SALVATION."

26
YOU DO NOT KNOW

You criticize the unfortunate woman who sells her body, trapped by the commerce of the flesh…

You do not know, however, the insanity and bitter agony lying beneath the make-up that covers her face.

Distraught, she believes that there are no other resources to acquire what is necessary for an honorable and simple life, or to support the sick relatives who know nothing about her plight.

You cannot pass judgement on the unfortunate people that pass you by.

Many of them ignore the abyss they live in. They are blind to the light because they were swallowed by the misfortune of their own invigilance.

You have no idea how much ignorance afflicts and hurts!…

Life has spared you from the siege of the wicked and the traps of constant ills.

You cannot imagine how much a burn hurts if you never experienced a red-hot iron touching your skin…

Extend your merciful hands like wings of love, and lift those who fell into the mires.

They are punished by the wounds they bear after their fall.

The defeated suffer while lying on the ground.

It is up to those who are standing to bend down and help them.

The light that helps plants grow does not inquire about the origin of the thornbush or disdains the den of jackals.

It warms, illuminates, and proceeds on its way…

You cannot foresee your tomorrow. And even if you could, you must still help today.

And even if you never need a pair of hands as helping levers, you can and should extend yours, because the pain of others will not allow you to be blissful —even if you try.

No one can be completely happy while tears still well up in the afflicted eyes of other people.

Your neighbor's house is an extension of your own. And the person that passes, humiliated and defeated, catching your attention, is something you cannot disregard.

Those who have not yet achieved total success do not know the extent of their personal resilience.

Remember that Jesus, at receiving the perfume from the woman of ill repute, did not inquire about its origin. Rather, He said, after a brief dialogue: *Go and sin no more,* offering her the chance to renew herself, which in turn became a living and active message to all of us.

27
TORMENTED SPIRITS

They proceed as if they were tethered to the afflictions they suffered in the flesh.

Their tormented, distorted features reflect their superlative anguish.

Half mad and blinded, they are still dominated by non-real pleasures.

They still have a fascination for shiny coins and piles of bills, sticking their hands in fetid mud that they confuse with imaginary gold.

They believe themselves to be thought leaders, afflicting incautious minds in lengthy processes of hypnosis, destabilizing the bodies and psyches of incarnate individuals.

They keep their lustful behavior, chasing mirages of their own insanity.

They shackle themselves to their personal opinions, impassioned and defeated by mental chains difficult to remove.

They remain attached to their decaying physical remains, far from any lucid discernment.

They embark in cruel undertakings, harboring sad ideas of revenge.

Shackled to all consuming hatred, they claim to have been cheated out of their earthly assets.

They believe to have been betrayed by those who remained in the flesh, so they become merciless persecutors.

Insane, they gather in groups of delinquents like clouds of horror, spreading untold restlessness and unbalance.

They ignore their own situation.

Stunned by the inevitable reality of disincarnation, which revealed immortality to them, they awaken unhappy, shackled to the same iniquitous goals they had while on the earth.

They bear very strong memories:

...As former wealthy people, whose unused possessions rust and rot;

...As enemies of other people's peace, since they never loved anyone;

...As winners at the game of the illusion, who remained distant from the truth;

...As thieves who stole the happiness of many, turning their home into a hell and their spouses into slaves.

They are the pleasure-seekers of all sorts who succeeded amid rivers of someone else's tears, advancing through hypocrisy in dishonorable maneuvers.

And, yes, they died... but they were not extinguished by the grave.

Life was waiting for them after death, along with the indestructible memories of their failed experiences...

They lost their equilibrium at the impact of a hounding conscience assaulted by horror, or by the remorse that becomes its own avenger.

Uneasy, they perturb and afflict all who identify with them through thoughts or actions.

Remember them with consoling compassion, and help them with your forgiveness.

Pray for them, as it will bring them comfort and hope.

All of them, just like you, will return to the purifying crucible of reincarnation.

No one is destined to endless unhappiness or punishment.

Our Heavenly Father is Magnanimity Itself and His Mercy is a sun that shines on and keeps all His children warm.

So, help them today, just like you were once helped by other hearts that you presently do not remember...

And, participating in their pain, be grateful to the Spiritist teachings that lifted the veil hiding reality beyond the grave, convening you to an honorable behavior and to serve a higher ideal.

It does not matter if you suffer following the righteous goal.

Do not complain about the agonies on the harsh path.

Do not irresponsibly believe that the pains and persecutions that reach your soul through mediumship, whether as spirit obsessions or mediumistic communications, can become a social pastime for idle hours, making you arrogant when you are summoned to the *evangelizing dialogue*[10].

Understand them and prepare yourself.

Though your young and vibrant body seems like a protective shield, disincarnation will also drag you into the grave. And if irresponsibility has marked your days on the earth –even as you pretend to ignore the truth that you learned while being in contact with the spirit world– you will become one of them. You will wander in a state of perturbation until, just like them, you will look for someone to extend to you their sincere help and Christian compassion.

---

10 A dialogue to enlighten discarnate Spirits exerting harmful influences on incarnate individuals. For more in-depth information see paragraph 249 of *The Mediums' Book* by Allan Kardec (International Spiritist Council). – Tr.

28
SERVE MORE

You feel the anguish in your soul like to a hopeless parasite embedded in a venerable oak tree, sucking away its vitality. You try to break free from this tenacious influence ravaging you in a prolonged siege. Work and serve more.

Active work in service of others turns into life-sustaining peace.

You feel your own fragility as you confront the cruel reality of a thousand hurts. You reach out for help and struggle without protection.

Work and serve more.

The dignifying work that you do in service to others becomes a safe harbor for your troubled heart.

You observe the unpredictable nature of everyday events, and you realize how little life's colors touch you. You harbor discouragement in the innermost recesses of your soul, and you let it consume the courage that you so much need.

Work and serve more.

Work is life, and service applied toward edification is the main beam supporting your happiness.

Wherever you might be, you will see suffering and adversity marching triumphantly over victims and ashes…

Work and serve more.

Service raised to the category of Christian duty, and work elevated to the condition of humanitarianism, become spiritual currencies for the acquisition of all the real necessities along the evolutionary journey.

Change the negative perceptions that darken your soul, and try to get to the bottom of life's problems rationally.

You will discover blessed fountains where you saw only swamps, if you try to remove the mud that obstructs the flow of pure water.

You will find fertility amid manure, if you mix the soil allowing life to manifest.

Happiness will replace boredom and sadness, if you turn on the light of personal joy, helping the propagation of hope for the good of all.

Thus, work and serve tirelessly.

Above the dark clouds the sun is shining.

Above the storm —in the upper layers of the atmosphere— all is calm.

There is always light and joy available to those who give themselves to renewing and edifying work, even if there is darkness all around them…

Learn to transform the difficulties that multiply in your life into opportunities to work and serve.

And, always remember Jesus Christ, the Tireless Servant. Honoring the quickly passing hours at the time of His testimony, He did not just call the thief to renewing work, but also all those who were gathered around the Cross —teaching without words— that service on the earth is the happy portal that leads to the Kingdom of Heaven.

29
TASKS

You would like to serve from a prominent position, eliminating many difficulties and solving the afflicting problems that affect the people.

You would like to tackle the big issues, eliminating all forms of crime. You would like to participate in special projects in the field of scientific research or social sciences, opening new frontiers for all.

You would like to work in the high spheres of religion, discussing the needs of the people with the governments of the world and proposing illuminating and liberating paths.

You would like to be a leader in the community, favored by the resources you see in others, and you lament their inefficiency …

However, you know nothing about the struggles in the frontlines.

Perhaps you are unaware that all of them –those invested with the responsibility to solve the problems of other men and women– are also human beings with problems.

They agonize, suffer, cry, and wear a mask over their faces, according to the customs of unfortunate politics or the standards of a decadent culture.

They fight against entrenched and odious systems.

They are often defeated.

They reached the heights of power without a safe foothold.

They are just like you.

A prominent position does not make for an upright conduct.

A change in government does not produce a sudden moral change.

The social problem is more complex than it seems.

But there is still a lot that you can do. Not from the top, but from where you are.

The sumptuous palace relies on the foundation that supports the construction.

If your current situation is not what you had hoped for, remember that the home is the first school for any future endeavor. All those who made their mark in the world first passed through the anonymous hands of parents and teachers, who devoted themselves to the task with major and untold sacrifices.

The humble tool that broke ground where the monument will one day stand is the sister of the chisel that sculpted the stone.

The simple hoe that prepares the soil is a companion to the pen that enacts the agrarian laws to ensure fair land distribution.

All tasks in the name of the good are divine ministries in which we must invest our vitality without weariness or complaints.

Without the hands of a humble cook, the hands of the wise could not propel human progress...

Thus, perform your duties with your soul in prayer. And although you do not enjoy notoriety in the world, remember Jesus –still the Great Anonymous Servant– who taught us that the greatest honor on the earth is the privilege to help and carry on, always serving without weariness.

30

IN THE WORK OF DISSEMINATION

Do not be discouraged in the dissemination of noble Christian principles because those who hear your words are distracted.

If the friend who seemed to be standing strong fell, lift him up, offer him your loving hands and comfort him once again.

If someone who was listening to you anxiously left to helplessly surrender to error, consider their carelessness and encourage them once more to fight against evil.

If sick persons who just regained their health went back to their old ways, distant from fellow workers and moral responsibilities, remind them of their commitments and duties once more.

If your companion looks bored and visibly fed up, renew his or her strength in the fountain of pure faith and keep helping.

If slander plunged a dagger into your heart, forgive the ungratefulness of those who receive your help and continue to lend assistance.

If wickedness ties you up to the post of affliction, examine your own attitude and continue to offer support.

When scorned, do not strike back but try to always be useful.

When insulted by those you love and teach, forget all offenses, and help without resentment.

The distracted are immature Spirits.

Persecutors are catalysts of various ills.

Mockers are not aware of themselves.

The imprudent are *spiritual children*.

The wicked become victims of their own behavior.

Amid all the desertions and failures —originated in the lack of strength that surrounds you— take heart in Jesus Christ. Remember that you are only a servant, engaged in a helping task, and that all results belong to Him —the source of all goodness. And after your hard toil, you will discover virtue and love in the recesses of your soul, resplendent like the light of God that illuminates you within.

31
OBJURGATORIES

You use the disappointment that characterized your religious experience, which afflicted you and broke your heart, to justify your current rebelliousness and desertion from the path of enlightenment.

You were looking for peace, but only encountered struggles.

You were hoping for tranquility, but only found disquiet.

You wanted health, but only met with disease.

You were waiting for help from above, but the Divine Ears seemed closed to your requests.

Thus, you say that it is only natural that rebelliousness took a hold of your heart.

You had a different idea in relation to Spiritism, but deception inevitably was the answer you got.

You are the only responsible party, however.

Faith is the lamp that shines within you. It is a journey, not a transport; a road, not a rest area.

Spiritism does not solve problems according to the deceptive observations you make on the earth.

For many, Divine Mercy should be a slave at the beck and call of all passions.

And yet, the best way to avoid certain diseases is *vaccination*.

For many instances, help still comes in the form of suffering.

God helps us, not the way we want, but according to our real needs.

For certain wounds, cauterization is still the most appropriate healing method…

So why make our Father or our faith into our servants –partial to us– transforming the justice of the Law that leads to our atonement into something negative or harmful?

Who is more deserving: those who ask for more, or those who work harder?

Thus, abandon unfair objurgatories and complaints and start serving.

A Spiritist commitment means connection with higher duties.

Spirit Guides and Mentors will not attend to your petty requests and solve problems that are yours to solve. However, they will give you – through wordless conversations and nameless stimuli– the harmony that is the path to genuine peace and happiness, away from pain, agony, and death, in the beautiful work that manifests itself in the everyday struggle.

32
PRESS ON

As you observe the obstacles hindering your march during the earthly journey, continue to work and serve. In them, you will find invitations to practice humility, chances to strengthen your perseverance, and calls to faith. You will understand the need to insist on doing the good; you will discover a wealth of joy in each victory, and you will engage in tireless work.

But do not stop your task halfway because it came easily to you.

The wind erodes the mountain that blocks its passage slowly and insistently.

The giant oak tree grows one cell at a time.

A monument is built stone upon stone.

What you cannot do right now, you will do later, if you persist in the endeavor.

The Gospel teaches that a servant should never be discouraged, even when apparently defeated. And Apostle Paul summons the people to proceed even with *lax knees*.

Do not adhere to the mindset of the defeated because, just like you, they are on an earthly journey, and their consciences will awaken one day to examine all their wasted opportunities.

If somebody tells you that your efforts are foolish, remain silent and insist on performing your duties.

If the acorn ever said that it would one day become a giant oak tree, no one would believe it.

Well before the eminent John Dalton conceived the *Foundations of Molecular Theory*, matter was already constituted by molecules.

If the humble and good earth should stop its blessed ministry of helping the seeds grow on account of the pessimists' predictions, humans and animals would die from scarcity. And if the delicate human embryo could hear you talk about the days lying ahead, it would think that you are crazy.

Thus, do not be intimidated by the information provided by unhappy people, who try to darken the sky of your hopes with dark and heavy clouds in the whirlwind of their lingering passions.

✳

You will continue to advance if you insist on a clear conscience, while doing your best.

And, if death interrupts your work, even so you will proceed indefinitely on the pathways of Eternity.

From the Higher Spheres, those who preceded you on their return to the spirit world —and continue to live— will come to dry your tears and console your heart. They will support your Spirit and sow happiness along your path during difficult times, so that you will not collapse in the middle of the fierce battle. They will cry and smile with you, confident and anxiously waiting to embrace you with the joy of someone who receives a relative coming back home after harsh battles...

Insist on your dedication to the good and press on, happy and confident, after all.

33
IN THE SOWING OF LOVE

Do not waste time analyzing other people's mistakes, because wrongdoers will answer for the time they used negatively.

Do not point to the thorns along the road, while keeping your distance from them.

Do not argue with evildoers, convinced of your own safety.

Do not doubt the power of prayer.

Do not create adversaries of your peace of mind, because hatred is a devastating fire.

Do not wait to be rich to do the good. A humble coin applied to charity is more valuable than a fortune lying dead in a strongbox.

Do not keep for your own gratification the excess that could mitigate the multiple needs of others.

Never lend assistance without the stimulating contribution of joy.

Do not apply the knowledge of the truth to show off or to afflict others.

Do not disdain the treasure of the minutes. Eternity is made of seconds.

Do not demand affection or applause to feed your vanity, even if everyone praises your excellent work.

Do not put out harsh or rigid programs if you cannot seal your words with good deeds.

Do not disdain other people's sweat that came as a result of struggle and pain.

Do not demand special preference.

Do not exhibit your deeds, even discreetly, because any good advertising loses credibility when it comes from an interested party.

Do not demand the presence of friends in places where your feet did not take you.

Do not let evil enter the realm of your soul.

Do not lend your ears to the racket of slander.

Do not assign importance to evil to the point of doubting the final and unquestionable victory of the good —as lived by Jesus, our Master and Lord.

34
THE MARKED

You approach the defeated in order to help.

Do not believe, however, the crushed to be just those who fall along the way, succumbing to discouragement and pessimism. Focus your attention, and with the eyes of the Spirit you will see that many of the defeated happen to be around you, projecting strength and being garrulous to conceal the signs of their unhappiness.

But if you are to love efficiently, you must love them.

Some are friends who are marked by moral mishaps and disasters, which the branding iron of the Divine Law has reached in order to eliminate their heavy debts…

Some are brothers and sisters marked by cruel diseases that ruined their digestive system, damaging their gastrointestinal tract…

Several are companions affected by physical ailments –concealed by expensive garments– that the eyes of the world cannot see, atoning for their past...

Several are the lonely hearts making amends in the grip of tormenting love experiences, renewing the landscape of a sick mind…

And many others are Spirits of different origins, perturbed by severe circumstances that incapacitate them, in silence, crushing their hope…

They all need balms for their painful marks, serving as purifying corrective measures.

When you come across them, do not torment them even more with unnecessary questions, twisting the knife of morbid curiosity in their wounds.

Time travelers on the earth, we all bear signs and marks that tear at the innermost fibers of our being.

Thus, before these marked people collapse, you can do something in their behalf. Later on, a new day will rise and another opportunity will arrive. And though you may be invited to help by praying, you are not able to foresee if, from one moment to the next, the Law may invite you to bear an even deeper mark…

35
EXPERIENCING TRIALS

You are waiting for happiness that seems late in arriving.
You yearn for total peace.
You long for harmony around your steps.
You hopelessly wish for fraternal understanding.
You fervently pray for help with your task.
Thus, no matter how harsh the struggle may be, wait with a robust faith.

✳

In the past, you sowed affliction in other souls.

At present, you harvest the thorns that look threatening.

Yesterday, you drowned the hopes of others in the mire of revenge, in rivers of blood and tears.

Today, it is necessary that you emerge with a purified conscience.

In the past, your greed seized the assets of many in coffers of usury, through illicit expedients.

At present, you must return them through arduous work and difficulties, along with payment of high-interest rates.

Yesterday, you encouraged hatred and erected monuments to pride and senselessness.

Today, it is natural that you are alone, surrounded by the aversion of many.

In the past, you allied yourself with crimes perpetrated by the powerful, with the illusion that life would go on forever.

At present, you suffer injustice and persecution wherever you go.

Before, you neglected even the smallest duties.

Now, you are fettered to heavy responsibilities.

✳

The Law establishes that no one will find peace without ennobling work.

No head will bear the crown of laurels over a polluted conscience.

Every ascent demands that we return to the very place where we failed.

No one will enter Heaven without having made amends on the earth.

The affliction that we impose on another is the affliction that we will bear in our own souls.

A crime committed casts a shadow on our path, waiting for the light of rehabilitation.

Irresponsible behavior in exchange for human success is an active debt in the Divine Ledger.

Those who have unpaid debts are slaves to the past, without the possibility to advance.

If you want to be free in the middle of the struggle, suffer patiently.

Pull out the thorn that you drove into another person's heart, at the price of your own sacrifice.

Fascinated by the promises of the future –even though you suffer– do not be afraid to go back and right your wrongs, enduring heroically the conditions for atonement as they unexpectedly disrupt your peace, attack your honor, get in the way of your success, bring anguish into your relationships, or cause persistent diseases in your aching body.

Do not stop, postponing long-awaited opportunities.

Other human beings, shackled to even greater debts, yearn for the opportunity you are now enjoying.

Facing even more dire perspectives, they would give their entire happiness to experience the great pain that is the harbinger of rehabilitation.

Thus, regardless of how somber your days may be, persist confidently and wait for the blessed day of liberation. Seek the Lord through prayer, and you will find the strength to persevere. Remain serene within and pray for the gift of peace in the future, being one with the pure and simple love that will elevate you to serve freely in favor of all those whom you owe.

36
IN HONOR OF THE GOOD

When Alexander the Great made his triumphant entrance in the city of Corinth, he noticed that Diogenes –the famous father of Cynic philosophy– was not present at the lavish banquet offered in his honor.

Because he was a great admirer of the strange philosopher, he set aside his self-professed self-importance for a moment and paid a visit to Diogenes in the humble abode where he passed his days immersed in deep reflection. To impress the illustrious cynic philosopher, Alexander offered him honors, glory, laurels, and triumphs. But, unperturbed before the conqueror of his land, Diogenes responded visibly annoyed "[do not] *take from me what you cannot give,*[11]" referring to the sunlight that the hefty body of the war hero was blocking.

You will be surprised to find people who offer you glory in exchange of favors; joy in exchange of gifts; money in exchange of subservience; and pleasure in exchange of moral degradation, but they can give you neither peace nor inner happiness.

Superficial gifts are fleeting.

Ornamental flowers are fragile.

Illusion turns into disappointment and gaping wounds that ooze continual bitterness.

Delectable liquor intoxicates and contributes to the unraveling of the body, pushing it closer to the grave.

---

11 "*I have nothing to ask but that you would remove to the other side, that you may not, by intercepting the sunshine, take from me what you cannot give.*" – Tr.

Meanwhile, without the laurels of the conquerors of the world, the Lord allows you to sow light, distributing with your own hands the ennobling concessions of perennial joy.

Even if you do not find souls willing to change direction and follow you, you can nonetheless instill color and beauty in their horizons with the premises of the Good News that illuminates you within.

When you find them rebelling against their existence, remind them of the long, sleepless nights that their parents spent watching over them when they were sick as little children...

Just as fire does not ask for fuel to be put out, a wound does not ask for the blade of a knife to heal.

You will discover Nature singing hymns of praise and hope, and paying homage to the good everywhere.

Clouds serve by creating fountains in rural lands.

Trees serve by providing shade, shelter, firewood, and fruit.

The sun tirelessly serves organized life on earth in the name of the Divine Sun.

Do not consider yourself on the sidelines of events, or covet the mirages of illusions.

When you extend your hands to help, raise your thoughts to the Higher Regions of Life and ask for assistance.

And do not allow other people's iniquity to rob you of what it cannot give you: the sun of belief and the warmth of hope.

The daughter of the widow of Nain, wrapped in mortuary cloth, had been defeated by death. But when the Master softly called her, she returned to active life to definitively prepare herself for the pilgrimage into the afterlife –something that would happen later due to the physical body's wear and tear...

37
EXAMINE AND MOVE FORTH

You sadly remember the desertion of the most dedicated fellow servants of the good.

You witnessed the fall of fervent idealists when their testimony required prayer and moral fasting.

You accompanied with concern the retreat of brothers and sisters who fought in the frontlines.

You cried bitter tears over the negative reaction of those you trusted most.

You heard the voice of anger come out of rebellious mouths, when otherwise calm individuals came undone before a difficult task.

You waited to no avail for the deserters to return to the edifying work, through which you serve the Divine Servant.

In the face of deceptions and difficult trials you declare yourself tired. You see shadows where there was bright light before; pessimism where there was hope; punitive affliction for the soul suffering self-renewal, and you feel you lack the strength to continue.

Everything seems to conspire against your lofty commitments: the incomprehension of some, difficulties with others, abandonment and loneliness.

However, you cannot postpone the need to move forth.

Faith has become a nourishment that you cannot be without.

All your plans for happiness were born of the faith that you have in your heart.

Listen to your own conscience, and you will understand how much it means to you.

Do what you can and always do your best.

The dark hour is an opportunity to turn on the light that begins to dim in many minds that were once illuminated by the flame of hope.

Search for enthusiasm, and your joy will once again be blessed with motivation.

The home will not strike you as a punitive penitentiary, but rather a school where you learn how to serve; your fellow companions will no longer look like deserters, but rather infirm individuals waiting for compassion and medication; those who persecute you will no longer look like enemies, but rather tormented beings held in the grip of cruel hands that afflict and perturb the lives of others; and the scarce resources will suddenly seem to be sufficient, because you will discover hidden treasures in the gifts of the Spirit...

Thus, even if the majority chooses a different line of conduct in the school of faith where you enrolled your Spirit, there is no reason to be discouraged.

At the right time, everybody will have to return the assets they have received and give an account of their usage.

The moment, at the height of your disappointments, can also be the instant that precedes the transition of your soul, as a natural imposition that life demands from both the absconders as well as the aspirants to the truth. And in the afterlife, all that you did, overcoming pessimism and mourning, pain and anguish —because you remained faithful— will be solace for your longing, happy security, and victorious peace.

Therefore, examine and move forth, under the inspiration on the good while you have the strength, so that in your twilight years you unveil a sunny path.

Remember that the Excellent Son of God, who was without error and had committed no crime —after having sown the unperishable good among unhappy and suffering people— saw His beloved friends desert in fear. He experienced injuries and curses, accepted vinegar and gall in the name of love, to become, after His *death,* a sublime flash of light pointing the way to the glorification that lies within the reach of all humankind.

38
WITH A TRUSTING SOUL

You remember them with tears in your eyes and an aching heart as if you were trampled on by a herd of wild horses.

Long-held hopes lay dead.

Precious and alluring promises look like a dark web of lies.

Loving friends have forgotten you.

A love that seemed eternal has fled.

Embraces and caresses have disappeared.

Gentle and extended hands are now hidden.

Companions that were the living example of loyalty have left you.

Honest deeds that cost you sweat and tears are now seen as the product of usury and are left to slowly rot.

At each moment, a new thorn pierces your flesh.

Ingratitude comes out of the mouth of those indebted to your love.

People for whom you sacrificed now complain about you.

Incomprehension comes from the very people who depended on you the most.

They all turn their backs on you or leave the room when you enter, and you feel like they are being unjust.

Even so, do not despair.

Contract your limp muscles, renew your tired Spirit, and proceed without dismay.

If you cannot harvest the blessed fruit of your efforts now, you will harvest them later.

What you are harvesting today, you planted yesterday.

Your present efforts will be tomorrow's credits.

Wrap your inner aspirations in the positive vibrations of tireless love, forgiving and edifying always, and let yourself be carried by the current of ennobling work, moving forth in your capacity as a sower of Eternity.

Losing everything, but having everything...

Persecuted, but never cross...

Injured, but jubilant...

Indicted, but innocent...

Tired, but standing up...

Beaten, but happy...

Falling to gather strength, rising reanimated to take the next step...

The language of the good possesses an undying vibration: it disappears here only to reverberate somewhere else.

What good you do is a gift that will make you better...

Have no regrets and do not lament.

And if it were necessary to die on the job amid anguishes and longings, seen as incapable and defeated, remember the Divine Master who, before achieving His eminent liberation, was persecuted and flogged, drinking the gall of human wickedness to the last drop and, carrying the infamous Cross all the way to Golgotha, reappeared soon thereafter in stellar glory, freed from dust and darkness...

39
... AND YOU WILL LIVE

Y ou are exhausted...
   Weariness, doubt, and misfortune are the expressions that keep
   your lips in mourning.

Discouraged by companions who have abused the generous fountain of your pure trust, you dare not embrace new activities.

You know, however, that discouragement is the implacable tenant of the Spirit.

You believe to have been abandoned, and fail to react.

You know that the sharp blade is not responsible for the cuts it makes... Yet you surrender this working instrument to rust without making the necessary effort to move it in the direction of edifying service...

You can always start over, dear friend.

Internalize the search for happiness and discover the treasures lying within your reach to help other people.

Your weariness is also the weariness of many of those who abandoned you...

Your doubt comes from the affliction caused by those who deserted your circle...

Your sorrow is the despair of those who capsized in the stormy sea of testimonies...

Do not think that you need to leave your house to help change the world.

First, renew yourself right where you live.

In your very home and on the very streets where you walk you will find a thousand opportunities for improvement.

Let good words rise from your lips; let the light flow from your eyes; let strength move through your hands; let love multiply in your heart, and you will distribute treasures benefiting those around you.

Though you do not know it, you are a teacher to other students.

People are watching what you do.

Affection is waiting for a chance to come into your life.

Happiness is not your enemy.

Go to those who cannot come to you.

Forget groundless resentments.

Those who hurt on purpose have an infirm mind.

Those who keep enemies ignore the laws of exchange that sustain life in Nature.

We all need something or someone to climb the steps on the ladder of spiritual ascension.

No Spirit will free itself from the earth on its way to a personal heaven for their own enjoyment.

Do not forget that the good you do is the only work that matters, and that the task you perform to benefit others is the only form of charity for yourself, capable of reaching the core of the soul, liberating it to join the ministry for the betterment of the world.

Ending the conversation with the priest that tried to trick Him, the Master said in the parable of The Good Samaritan *"Go and do likewise!"*

Do not miss an opportunity to help just because weariness, doubt, and misfortune insist on taking a life of their own to dominate your soul, smothering it with the powerful tentacles of pessimistic affliction.

Overcome all evil and you will live.

40

HEROES

They go unnoticed in their anonymous daily tasks, creating happiness all around them.

Humble mothers who work very hard at household chores, tending to multiple responsibilities to teach and confer dignity to their children in search of learning and work opportunities...

Many hearts offer their charitable hands to lend assistance and care to others...

Anonymous workers who tire themselves in their daily toil to put bread on the humble family table...

Obscure sanitation workers, assailed by disease, struggling to sustain the honest home where they perform the sublime task of raising a family...

Lively young girls that blush when embarrassed, working menial jobs to care for their sick mothers lying on miserable cots...

Young people who study at night after a hard day's work in order to progress in life...

They are everywhere, lost in the crowds, ignoring their own worth.

On their silent renunciation, the Christ is establishing new bases for hope, giving rise to the realms of true happiness.

But there are other types of heroes too!

Acclaimed by the world, they enjoy the respect of the masses, and their passage marks the epochs in which they lived.

Some worked in research, and gave everything to save humankind with the product of their tireless, dedicated investigations.

Others worked silently in hospitals, offering their skilled hands in delicate surgeries that saved lives from the grip of death.

Some saw their hair turn gray while bending over books, enabling knowledge to penetrate the souls, educating, guiding, saving...

They are the engineers and clergy, lawyers and scientists, statesmen and legislators, changing the face of the earth and keeping the social peace on which to build a new society.

There are also the heroes returning from the battlefront, scarred by grenade and mortar shrapnel, hurt or disturbed, after having taken part in horrible battles through which they sought to preserve the dignity and the peace of those who remained at home with their families...

All of them, however, in need of peace, love, and understanding...

All of them men and women that circumstances placed on the pedestal of fame or the sacrificial pyre, in order to do the Heavenly Father's work among the creatures of the earth.

If you know them, pray for them and show them respect; if you meet them, think of their example and show your appreciation; if you know their names, love them despite the distance, helping them with your esteem. They also love, smile, cry, and suffer...

Some —notable souls imprisoned in the flesh— clear the path for human beings and human thought; others —resolute Spirits embarked in critical atonements— provide higher lessons of exemplification and duty. But they all work on behalf of the Greater Life so that the language of the good will not disappear without echoing its message among the afflictions of the earth.

If possible, do not disturb them, but rather help them finish the tasks they dedicate themselves to, fulfilling their duties for their own happiness.

After becoming famous, Mme. Curie had to emphatically turn away inopportune people and admirers from her home, so she could continue to study and work on *radium* —expanding the knowledge of physics— and ultimately succumbing to it, but at the same time saving millions of lives.

Help them as well.

41
AFFLICTION

Bless difficulty and incomprehension on the road you travel alongside other souls.

The small bird experiences affliction inside the constrictive eggshell that gave it life to fly towards infinite horizons.

The humble plant embryo experiences affliction inside the bursting seed to then grow into a big tree on the surface of the earth.

The stream of water experiences affliction as it squeezes through the fissure in a rock to then run free over the great valley.

The rose bud experiences affliction, folded onto itself, to then bloom and spread its scent everywhere.

The caterpillar experiences affliction, immobilized during histolysis, so that the colorful butterfly may glide in the balmy air of a springtime morning.

The soul experiences affliction inside the cocoon of flesh to then one day reach the horizons of eternal life.

It is necessary, however, to deeply examine the nature of our own afflictions.

Afflictions that transform life and elevate.

Afflictions in breaking the ties that bind the Spirit to crime, enabling freedom.

Afflictions in imparting light within ourselves, creating enlightenment.

Afflictions in communicating the truth, causing hearts to rejoice.

Afflictions in forgetting wrongs, spreading serenity and joy.

Afflictions in overcoming difficulties, fostering projects for the practice of edifying deeds.

Afflictions in making good use of time, appreciating the blessing of the hours.

... And then there are afflictions that express insanity and death.

Affliction for a freedom that is debauchery.

Affliction for a pleasure that destroys inner peace.

Affliction for love that represents animalistic passions.

Affliction for money that represents a gilded cage.

Affliction for power that turns into madness.

Affliction for glory that becomes an accomplice to crime.

Affliction for deceptive honors, resulting in ridicule and farce.

Affliction for hatred, which turns into a deadly poison.

Afflicted individuals and worried individuals.

Those afflicted in search of peace.

Those worried about the torments of *death*.

Tormented souls and Spirits thirsty for life have always existed.

With Jesus, we learn how to free ourselves from all torments and how to endure all afflictions.

Afflictions born in the labyrinths of the Spirit.

Afflictions originating in the abyss of other people's passions.

Restlessness of the inquiring "I".

Concerns over someone else's disquiet.

Preserve your peace when the afflicted world summons you to the realm of the unbalanced, and continue fighting to find the inalienable treasures of the Kingdom of God.

Give yourself over to God, keeping your peace for suffering afflictions but not causing them, remaining faithful and steadfast in the practice of the good until your disincarnation.

And ultimately victorious —enjoying the peace that emanates from Him— you will see proof of the gift of immortality, confirming His unforgettable statement:

"Blessed are those who mourn, for they shall be consoled."

42
PRUDENCE

Turn to prudence whenever difficulty points you in the direction of perilous paths.

Difficulty is not just the obstacles ahead, hindering your march.

There are many difficult problems manifesting as a mad ambition, or a desire for triumph that becomes a vehicle for indulgence.

You will find people with problems despite having large sums of money at their disposal, as well as those living in torment for lacking the most basic resources.

Prudence will tell you that those who hoard resources succumb dominated by the dead and stagnant assets that enslaved them, and you will remember that many crimes are the product of heartless aggression and mental insanity, because it was thought that money would be the solution to all their problems.

Thus, guard yourself in the position of someone who really wants to make the right decisions.

If you are not loved, love for the pleasure of loving.

If you are unable to fulfill your dreams, be content with the way things are.

If nobody helps you, help in any way you can.

Take advantage of all the lessons with which life honors your hours.

Anxiously giving in to impulsive behavior is like planting thorns on the very path you will have to walk on.

To try to solve a problem when we are emotionally unwell is like pouring acid on an open wound.

Let prudence's advice save you from a life of crime.

Tomorrow, you will repay life's loans in either transient resources or in rectifying trials in the name of our Father, for the only quantifiable values that follow us after death are the actions for which we will be known in the great dawn after our protracted sleep.

43
REQUESTED PRAYERS

Not just prayers for you.

Prayer should not be converted into an easy-to-swallow pill that friendly and easy assistance puts within the reach of our digestive system.

To pray is to become involved.

If you do not develop *antennae* in the recesses of your being to receive the comforting energy that is generated by the prayers that others make on your behalf, it will be like beneficial moisture falling on non-porous, compacted soil.

Traditional religions have taught us that in praying we conjugate the verb *to ask*. They forgot, however, that for a request to be considered, the petitioner must have essential merits, without which the Heavens remain silent…

Nonetheless, divine silence does not always mean that the petitioner is not being considered.

It's just that heavenly wisdom responds according to the real needs of the soul, as opposed to a person's apparent wishes.

In that sense, prayer cannot get lost in repetitive and mystic religious formulas, or in mechanical short pleas. Prayer must be worked in the recesses of the legitimate aspirations in life, in manifestations of the Spirit as an extrasensory element in which life's legitimate aspirations come through, in manifestations of inner enrichment, connected to the powerful sources of the Divine Majesty.

Do not simplify the problems in your life by asking others to pray for you. You would be overburdening them with the bread that is your task to attain, for the spiritual nourishment that you keep postponing.

Prayer is personalized sustenance.

Each person prays in the way they can, feel, and vibrate.

The Father, however, responds according to the merits, the needs, and the sincerity of the request.

And when someone acts like the man of Cyrene and extends their arms toward you to deliver the sublime response –like a celestial messenger– do not think that you possess merits that you fully know not to have, but remember the *profuse mercy* of our Father. And when someone asks you to have mercy and compassion, do to them as the Heavens did to you. Keep praying with feelings, transforming your own acts into a soft melody of prayer.

44
TOLERANCE

There is much talk about tolerance.

We preach about the need to practice this divine precept.

We write about the value of such a noble helper of love.

Tolerance, however, is seldom practiced.

Without it, we all know that beauty itself imparts sadness, and the chalice of success turns into a cup of bitterness, where boredom lingers.

But when the chance to practice it finally arrives, we allege that it is difficult.

When a person hurts another because they are in fact not well, our immediate response is: *We cannot allow such outrage to continue.*

Some dirty the floor out of ignorance; others insist on their requests because they are ill-mannered; some are annoying, not knowing what they are doing; others persecute, dominated by their own unhappiness; some run over others, controlled by evil forces; others make mistakes out of stupidity; some are disrespectful, besieged by their own primitive nature… And yet, few believers and proponents of tolerance are forgiving.

Seeking to justify their unmerciful attitude, they affirm that it is necessary to maintain order and encourage discipline.

If someone is late, reproach soon lashes out, forgetting the possibility of traffic congestion.

If the attire is inappropriate, criticism comes quick, ignoring the circumstances around that choice.

If a neighbor is loud, he or she is soon labeled as impolite, when in reality it could be the result of a spirit obsession.

If the boss is tough, right away he or she is seen as an enemy, forgetting that they also serve.

Every reaction is born with the acquiescence of reason, which in turn adapts to the justifications of the unbalanced mind.

Those who react have lost the strength to act.

Tolerance is not just a beautiful theoretical path: it is an active guideline.

Without those who make mistakes, there are no opportunities to practice tolerance. And how would we know if we have a tolerant behavior if we do not call it into action?!

Careless, silly, demanding, and cunning people are indispensable for tolerance to shine in the heart.

✳

A pious saint on an evangelical mission was assaulted by robbers who stole his belongings. After taking everything he owned, they beat him and chased him away...

Nonetheless, after a few minutes the humble and beaten man returned.

When asked why he had come back, he replied that he still had a gold coin in the hem of his tunic for emergencies, which the robbers had failed to take.

And, with a simple gesture, he gave it to them and then calmy and happily went about his way.

Moved to the core, the robbers became his disciples, after asking him to talk to them about his happiness and faith.

Tolerance loses and gives, suffers and forgives –paraphrasing Saint Paul's words regarding charity. It does not get mad, it does not curse, it does not suffer, it does not offend or hurt. It always helps, ready to serve, turning on the bright light of love in every heart.

45
APPEARANCES

Leave the study of the Gospel's texts to the exegetes. Seek to live according to the teachings of the Lord.

Avoid religious arguments. Join the work carried out in the name of faith.

Leave those who quarrel over the ministry of the Good News. Join those who produce in the name of fraternity.

Move away from demands in the realm of belief. Materialize with your hands the concepts to which you adhere on behalf of the people.

Argumentative individuals deserve no attention.

They do not disseminate light.

They do not fulfill the duty of lending assistance.

Their weak actions do not reflect their strong words.

They confuse, perturb, and create difficulties.

Verbalists can be compared to those fast-growing weeds that asphyxiate the weaker plants looking for an opportunity to live.

They proffer subtle destabilizing concepts, and become skilled in the art of distressing.

They are bearers of disquiet.

They sow doubts that create division.

They waste the treasure of time in long, pompous, and extravagant sermons.

Their hands are empty of Christian deeds, and their minds are filled of well-crafted concepts.

They dwell on details, and no imperfection gets past them.

They shine, but fade.

They succeed, but disappear.

Because they know that their kingdom is nothing but fiction, they are intractable, arrogant, and pretentious.

They believe to be ahead of their time, above and beyond the understanding of their contemporaries. That is why they escape into magnificent libraries, emerging only to criticize, lash out, and argue...

They die as they have lived, without finding self-realization.

The remembrance of them brings discomfort.

The world forgets about them and their memory disappears, because they left no relevant work behind.

They wake up in the afterlife, raggedy and tormented, amid memories of intellectual dreams and the sad vision of their shameful reality...

Do not forget to imprint the evangelical teachings into the folds of your heart.

Live as much as possible the examples of the verb to love. Just as the physical body gives you form, the divine message also gives form to the teachings of the Lord who, in silence, gave His testimony of loyalty to duty and love until the very end.

You will come before the codes of the Divine Justice with the list of your deeds speaking for you, and not your vehement words regarding wishes of never-realized accomplishments.

46
LISTEN AND ACT

Free yourself from the bitter memories that shackle you to the dark paths of the past. Listen to the call of the Messengers of the Truth. Offer your personal effort in the service of the general good on the common path of duty. And get into the thicket to clear productive patches of land, which will take care of you tomorrow.

Do not stop to examine your own affliction, imbued with negativity and unproductiveness.

The most useless water is the one that becomes stagnant sitting on mud, and the most inefficient worker is the one that does not try to produce.

Take advantage of the opportunity and use the time that you have available to steep your mind in optimistic, self-renewing, and active thoughts.

The spring that deeply penetrates the soil becomes enriched by the water table that increases its volume.

Do not give yourself over to lamentation by saying, *I'm unhappy!*

And do not cancel out the call by saying, *Who am I to help?*

Those who decree their own uselessness do not know themselves.

The humble seed does not become a tree by focusing on the negatives. It allows the knowledgeable farmer to put it into the appropriate type of soil to unfold its potential.

Become a seed for the active good, and do not be obstinate or demanding.

You are in the right place, at the right time, and have the necessary resources.

Pick yourself up and try to start something.

Reclaim your joy, and let hope turn on the light in the dark sky of your soul.

No one will ever reach the Spiritual Heights without sacrifice, or will find justification in failure by saying, *I could not!*

Everyone is endowed, not only with the resources that they deserve, but also with the possibilities that are most useful to them.

If birds were afraid to fly because of the abysses down below, they would remain immobilized in their own smallness, never experiencing the thrill of the open skies.

Thus, heed the sublime calling and start now.

If you fail, start over; if you fall, get right back up. Every moment is a valuable tool with which to perform the sacred task of trying to start over with Jesus.

Saints and heroes of the Higher Spirituality once experienced the same moments of indecision and suffering.

Those who believed in parasitic sanctification are still analyzing, their arms paralyzed, alongside hearts that are overwhelmed by superlative affliction.

Very appropriately, St. John Chrysostom once said *A sad saint is a sorry saint.*

So, regain your inner composure and accept the challenge of the honorable invitation by tackling any area of service.

Elevate your heart with the guidelines of Jesus, the Eternal Worker. Follow Him who summons us to life. Renew yourself in the work that transforms sinners and affords them communion with the angels, while other individuals –rich in faith and possibilities– stay behind, lingering in uselessness, engaging in transcendent but paralyzing contemplation.

47
IF YOU WANT TO

Once you start your incursion into the realm of the soul you will discover how hard the task really is.

Renunciation and loneliness, silent suffering and incessant effort are indispensable for the success of this undertaking.

However, if you want to fight against the germs of vice that consume you, you will gain a robust health that will never leave you…

You will be able to break the bars of the golden prison that vigorously enslaves you, accessing the vastness of freedom…

You will traverse the swamplands of pride and laziness, reaching the highlands of duty where simplicity lives.

You will forgive all evil, doing good to all those who do not understand you, and you will distribute the bright light of faith that fuels all your yearnings…

You will chase away fear and uncertainty, broadening the horizon of endless service…

You will discover treasures within yourself awaiting the decision of your will.

There are many brothers and sister begging for help who fell as they were crossing the marshlands of pleasure; who are caught in the thick ropes of uncertainty; who hold on to the fragile vessel of youth; who are lost in the labyrinth of anxiety; who consume themselves in the flames of lower desires; who poison themselves in the toxicity of hatred; who asphyxiate themselves in the fumes of lies; who writhe in the mud of lust; who deplete themselves in the tough path of crime; who get tangled up in the web of slander; who went insane in the arms of ambition. But, unfortunately, they remain there because they want to…

If you want to, you will move forward.

Individuals strengthen their muscles in the activities of their choice.

Irrigating the planted fields, the stream ignores how far its water will run.

Emitting its scent, the rose ignores how far the winds will carry it.

If you want to —even if you ignore the length of the path to be treaded— you will proceed, fighting with yourself, defeating every difficulty, and creating an atmosphere of love wherever you go.

You will then understand how Jesus —although martyred— was able to forgive His executioners and broaden the possibility to love, caring for the condemned thieves who kept Him company at the extreme hour. And like Him, you too will devote all your love to the glory of serving and growing, as the basis for the legitimate happiness set in the core of all hearts.

48
THE CURRENCY
OF GOODNESS

Convert the humble currency of your goodness into a repository of light that you will put within the reach of those who suffer.

Because of it you will discover valuable resources that can be transformed into joy for many beings.

Although deprived of money, you will see wealth losing its worth because it is not being put to good use.

The very eyes that afford you the blessed ability to enjoy colorful landscapes could read a page of evangelical consolation to those who are ignorant, translating the symbolic message that is veiled by the words.

With them, you can guide a blind person on a public street, saving them from the dangers of crossing busy intersections.

With your healthy and nimble hands, you will remove pestilent stagnant waters, eliminating breeding grounds for dangerous diseases.

You will give a new purpose to the ground, covering it with productive plantings, multiplying vegetables and grains that will grace many tables.

You will sew warm clothing to cover the ashamed nakedness of so many.

You will mend torn clothes to make them useful.

You will straighten crooked tree branches; you will carry things too heavy for small children and the elderly by just moving those helping tools that are your hands…

With your voice, you will exalt the Truth by speaking about the harmony of love.

You will defend outraged honor.

You will offer fraternal advice.

You will sing the song of hope.

You will bless...

Just with those resources alone from a strong body, you will be able to be a source of mercy to those defeated in the human struggle.

With your intelligence applied to solidarity as a simple duty, you will lift minds and hearts to the glorious higher realm of happiness.

With your affection, you will gift the angel of friendship to the bitterness spreading through the masses, and you will rekindle the light of understanding amid the darkness of devastating rebellions.

You will become an indefatigable source of goodness, spreading comfort and courage along the vast path of the souls...

We can always do something for other people.

Misery sees your abundance.

Rebellion sees your serenity.

The suffering world, crying tears of agony, listens to your jubilant hymns.

Why hold back your generosity?

The mercy you offer somebody else converts into tranquility for yourself.

The benevolence you provide to others blooms in your heart as perennial happiness.

And the forgiveness you give to those who offend you will become a song of peaceful blessings in the sublime conscience of life.

Thus, place the currency of goodness in your hands that otherwise has no worth, and help without restriction.

49
ABOUT PRAYER

Most believers expect to find in prayer a vehicle to eliminate pain that seems otherwise unsurmountable.

They pray for the same reasons they eat: to live well.

But, unlike food, prayer is a stimulus to help men and women live rightly. It is a vehicle of light and nourishment for life.

When the soul manages to maintain a prayerful state, it does not ask for anything, it gives of itself.

It does not ask to be freed from suffering, because in suffering it finds a corrective lesson and a way to right past wrongs. Prayer then becomes rational and objective. It leads the confident soul to the sources of life, providing it the strength to endure the burden it must carry.

Prayer builds the bridge or communication tool that enables the talk with the Lord, instead of just offering inspiration for a petitioner to break free from the burden imposed by the Lord.

Prayer can be compared to a hoe intensely working the soil where one intends to sow. It is necessary to use it wisely.

It would be pointless for farmers to beg the soil to open itself up so that they may scatter their productive seeds. And it would be equally pointless to beg the Divine Mother to extend her blessings without the strenuous effort that earns the necessary credits.

Thus, search for the sublime heart of Jesus reaching it with the blessed resource of your prayer; make an effort and, through Him, the seeds of the Heavens will be transformed, providing you with the necessary bread for a happy life during your earthly struggles.

Pray and endure your pains.

Pray and accept the necessary corrections.

Pray and try to find the strength to go on.

By praying, you will reach the Lord, who gave you in prayer a sure way to communicate with God's Infinite Goodness, in whose bosom you will quench the thirst of your afflicted Spirit...

50
HUMILITY

Humility, humility!...

Humility is an ignored virtue. And, for that reason, it is neither arrogant nor delusional.

The more it conceals itself, the more beautiful it gets. And, when ignored, it is like the brilliant dawn opening the day to the sun.

Humility is spontaneous and, to be genuine, it cannot be improvised. It must be cultivated with perseverance and developed tirelessly.

Wherever its first manifestations appear, you will also encounter powerful adversaries.

Modern life with its false notions conspires against its vitality, claiming it to be cowardice and weakness...

Humility, however, cannot be confused with shyness or fear.

It is not a static, but rather a dynamic virtue. For that reason, it is neither parasitic nor accommodating.

It is an active, combative force.

Only well-tempered characters can feel it.

To suffer with humility does not mean to give in to pain, but rather to fight heroically to defeat affliction without rebelling.

It is easier to avenge an offense than to forgive it, silencing all the inferior impulses that reside in our core.

When humility submits to the strong and rebels against the weak, it changes its character, degenerating into servility. On the other hand, it remains silent when accused by the powerful or when offended by the weak.

Humility helps without being smug about it, like a precious brook that does not know the benefit it spreads, like a smiling sun that is oblivious to the life it brings, like a blessed fruit that is not aware of its delicious taste...

✳

If you are being flogged by the forces of rebellion and if you are being hurt by the thorns of despair, sow humility in your heart today.

Perhaps tomorrow, you will continue to be the same. But the day will come when the excellent blessing of virtue will germinate and bloom in your life.

Trust and wait, and serving without fear you will experience the harmony that comes from enduring everything with humility out of love for the Great Love of all loves.

51
FACING DIFFICULTY

In order to free the plant contained inside itself in germ-like form, the seed endures the pressure of the soil…

The river in search of the sea does not stop in front of the obstacles that impede its flow…

Difficulty, therefore, is a test of resilience in the form of encouraging opportunities.

If pain –in any of its multiple modalities– visits your heart, stop for a moment and pray to replenish your Spirit. Through the soothing power of prayer, the heavenly resources will reach your mind, reinvigorating the fibers of life for the continuation of the journey.

Receive difficulty as an opportunity to do battle.

Accept pain as a messenger of awakening.

Embrace trials with joy.

Consider a problem as a test of the skills you have learned.

Listen to the cries of persecution with the ears of understanding.

And if it were necessary to endure all kinds of pain in order to test the excellence of your convictions in Jesus Christ, do not recoil.

Remember the *Via Dolorosa* –which is not just a demonstration of evangelical tragedy, but a vehement appeal that reverberates throughout the centuries– and answer the misunderstood signals calling you.

Winners on the earth are but deceived hearts.

Those who smile on the earth are but immature brothers and sisters.

The happy people of the earth are equally mistaken souls.

The true heroes on the earth are those who, anonymously and humbly, became bread to empty stomachs, clothes to naked bodies, shelter to homeless souls, clarity to those lingering in darkness, and hope to those bewildered by fear and paralyzed by imbalance.

In the face of the pain on the earth, there is no room for complaints, lamentations, or slander.

Do your duty.

If you are waiting for human understanding, you will only experience discomfort and disappointment.

But if you wish to serve the Lord and Master of us all, strive to overcome your greatest difficulty: the selfishness that is the source of pride and the fuel for other evils.

Rise above all vicissitudes, and remaining loyal to yourself in the fulfillment of the greatest duty, you will achieve a peaceful conscience after the victory over your difficulties.

52
BENEFACTORS

Because the splendors of the Spiritist teachings have filled your heart with happiness, you would like to serve courageously and even give your own existence for the sublime manifestation of the Good.

Having now discovered the beautiful side of all things and having confirmed that the Divine Wisdom has structured everything as it should be, you feel the need to share the happiness that enriches your life by spreading the light of love among all of God's creatures.

You are fascinated by the role of benefactor, and you affirm that you would give everything to become a messenger of the good in the struggle for sublimation.

The possibilities for you to offer your help are many.

Any help given is also a blessing that multiplies many times over. However, in order to help in a way that will benefit you in turn, a major work within yourself, at the core of the Spirit, is necessary.

Any noble act of giving is a sowing of light.

However, for the seed to attain the plenitude of the embryo, it is constrained to free itself from its own shell, transforming it into vitality.

For you to reach your goal you must also break through the shell of the "I", destroying the tower of granite where you house your individualism.

No one can serve well if expecting a reward of any kind.

For a spring to quench someone's thirst, the water rids itself from the mud at the bottom.

For bread to be served at the table, the wheat overcomes the dirt that surrounds its roots.

We do not properly serve if we offer love with acrimony and sourness.

Little does it matter that we renounce the pleasures of the world in favor of the work of the good, if our attitude will discourage the spontaneous manifestation of innocent and youthful joy on the part of those we help.

Genuine renunciation ignores the dimension of its own sacrifice. To be noble, it must be jovial and communicative.

To help while we complain can be compared to offering fresh water to the thirsty in a dirty glass.

To work while we are annoyed, weary and sullen, always gives the impression that we are performing a task under duress.

The work of The Lord is done with joy.

The sun smiles kindly to the swamp, without hurry or reticence.

The tree blesses people with shade and fruit, unaware of its own worth.

The rain tends to the soil without a problem, pouring over the valley as well as the mountain.

They all ignore the benefit they distribute.

In the past, it was thought that sanctification resulted from an austerity that made the face look gaunt, mortifying the body. With Spiritism, austere persons are not those whose lips are always stiff and frowning deforms the face...

We cannot help while cursing the help we give.

So, sprinkle the *salt of love* in the work that you do to keep the Christian flavor always present in your plate of solidarity.

If you want to serve successfully, observe the Messengers of the Divine Light and do likewise.

They never complain; they serve always.

They never demand; they understand always.

The never perturb; the appease always.

In any situation, they always reflect the bosom of an understanding mother or the arm of a strong father, offering consolation or work.

Benefactors, in a real sense are those who, forgetting about themselves, bear the crosses of other people upon their injured shoulders, and walk alongside them, without thinking of their own sacrifice.

On the *Via Dolorosa*, Jesus forgot about His own wounds and the offenses received from everyone to be able to make it to the end of the tragedy in the name of love. And He begged the Supreme Father —at the height of His afflictions— to forgive us, who even to this day —after two thousand years— continue to be unworthy servants of His Divine Message.

53
TRIALS

Before the delicate vase became an exquisite element of decor, skillful hands shaped the humble clay and baked it in fire.

The valuable telescope that brings the galaxy plunged in the celestial abyss closer, endured high temperatures and spent long months cooling off slowly.

For the metal blade to withstand the dangerous invasion of moisture that destroys it, it endured oxidation in high-temperature furnaces.

For the delicate jewel to become a priceless accessory, the gold was carefully purified by fire.

For electricity to illumine, delicate filaments inside a lightbulb become heated until they glow.

Fire is present in multiple processes within the scope of human activity and life in general.

Fire in the infinite sky: new suns, new incandescent worlds; fire on the earth: deadly lava, molten magma in the pyrosphere; fire in the soul: open wounds of torn emotions and a lacerated body…

The trials of an incarnate Spirit are a purifying fire.

Pain in the soul, in the form of anguish and longing, testing the resilience of faith.

Pain in the body, in the form of oozing wounds, testing the value of faith.

Emotional pain, in the form of anxiety and frustration, testing faith itself.

Nonetheless, from all struggles and trials the soul comes out purified for the innumerable glories of Immortality, just like gold comes out of its impure gangue to the splendor of a crown and the fineries of gold smithery.

During times of trial, seek shelter in the haven of patience, trusting your Heavenly Father.

Even if it is pouring difficulties, your days are marked by loneliness and your soul is ablaze –preventing your eyes from seeing the luminosity of the sun– trust in the Lord and keep going.

Those who have preceded you in the journey and today are your Spiritual Guides experienced the same afflictions in the past. They underwent their own trials, but overcame themselves, raised their hearts to the Love of God, and reached the pinnacle of redemption. And although their hearts were crushed, and their hands were hurt, their souls were anguished, their dreams were shattered, they awoke in the afterlife fully redeemed and infinitely happy.

54
THE BRIDGE

They stayed behind.

They could not keep up with the rhythm imposed by renewal.

While the Wise Messengers, like storytellers, spoke about celestial constructions, they listened spellbound. They liked the possibility of easy triumphs and could picture themselves crowned with success in the struggles of the common path, without putting forth any real effort.

They thought Spiritism was only a Consoling Doctrine, whose mission was limited to gathering sufferers and beggars to encourage them, drying their tears without any commitment to work and sacrifice, by which people become integrated into the movement to liberate consciences.

They forgot that physical death is not the end.

They forgot that, beyond the grave, there is neither rest nor a paradise but for those who converted their own peace into peace for others, and saw their happiness as the happiness of all.

After death, they will see that there is no definitive solution for the problems that reincarnation did not solve.

The earth is a great arena of work waiting for the dedication of those who toil on behalf of hope, truth and the good.

No one will transcend the earth in a state of liberation if they still have commitments from the past.

Those who stayed behind prefer fantasy and illusion.

They became the apologists of heroism without effort, expecting the glories of a job sponsored by earthly godfathers, the fleeting bearers of social and political prestige.

They pushed aside gigantic problems that they will have to face later, even more complicated and harder to resolve.

They retreated when it was time to advance, and stayed at a distance…

Do not criticize or lament them.

They are weak souls, incapable of a greater resistance.

With the hands of a devoted and gentle mother, Life —the great teacher— will gradually lead them bach to reality, from which no one escapes with impunity.

Keep moving.

Forget the fantasy of attractive narratives, and go out into the arena that is full of needs waiting for your collaboration.

Build a water fountain, and the desert will become an orchard.

Drain a stagnant swamp, and it will turn into a plentiful vegetable garden.

Remove the stones, and an easy road will open up for humans and animals.

Do the good everywhere with your hands and heart, praying and enlightening, so that the work of the truth will shine in your arms like brilliant stars in the shape of hands.

And, connected with the Spirits of Light, you will build —with your sweat and incessant effort while you remain in the flesh— a bridge over the abyss that you will soon cross —dazzled and elated— in search of the jubilant loved ones waiting for you on *the other side*.

55
WORK WITH WHAT YOU HAVE

Now that the clarions of truth reach your spiritual ears, conveying the blessings from the Heavens, you want to help the tormented people of the earth.

You wish you had the gift of the gab to reach the masses through the written or spoken media.

You feel the pain of many who are sick and, afflicted, affirm that you would help them if you possessed healing mediumship.

You try to elucidate those who stop to listen, but often times feel defeated because you cannot mediumistically register the Voices that provide information and revelation.

And you say in disappointment, *I do not see, I do not hear, I do not write, I cannot do anything…*

Do not believe, however, that the divine ministry of love in the world depends on having exceptional resources.

The great missionaries ignored their own worth.

Even when they reached the height of their sublime tasks, they never abandoned their humble jobs of so much value.

Talented human beings always existed on the earth, but they did not change the world for the better.

It was those who loved a lot, however, that became a compass, remedy, clarity, and safety for all.

So do not wait for perfection in order to help and guide.

Before practicing medicine, the future doctor works as a nurse, and no captain ever began in a position of command, bypassing key roles on the lower decks of the vessels.

Do the good to someone, discretely.

Not everyone will be able to accept you right away.

It also took time for you to accept the guidelines that direct your life today.

Proceed consoling the souls that you meet or who find you along the way, and as long as it is possible, disseminate the truth and do the good.

British poet John Keats, who succumbed to tuberculosis at the age of twenty-five, received death joyously…

The confident Titian proved his consummate mastery by continuing to paint at the age of ninety-four.

John Milton did not stop working because he became blind…

Though he suffered from left hemiplegia, Pasteur never lost heart…

Thackeray wrote with *spirit*, even though his beloved wife was insane…

Steinmetz, despite having *his* body *contorted by a hump in his back* and a crooked gait, performed true prodigies in the field of science.

Handel, impoverished and half paralyzed, worked intensely so that the *Messiah* –with its Halleluiah Chorus– would dazzle the world…

Jesus Christ –the Servant par excellence– rejected those holding titles and possessions to summon *simple and unrefined men* for the dissemination of the Kingdom of God on the earth. He reached the height of His messiahship through the dialogues maintained with the suffering hearts that sought Him out in secret, during the beautiful days of the dissemination of the Good News.

And even today, when the light of Spiritism permeates God's children renewing them inside, He continues to summon helpers who know how that, above them, it is the light of hope that must shine, motivating human life to keep advancing toward the love of Our Father.

56
CONFIDENT SERENITY

Let yourself be carried by the living waters of serenity, certain that you will reach the blessed harbor of your sublime destination.

Steer past the boulders in the form of failure and lower desires, attached to the reeds of depressing diseases that many times entangled you in the middle of the journey.

The more you focus on evil, the stronger it gets.

Concentrating on the mud at the bottom of the well degrades the pure water that continues to be rejected.

Likewise, when a disease-breading swamp is drained, it becomes a welcoming parcel of land ready to produce for the benefit of the community.

If you ponder about what the fertilizer is made of, you will feel nauseous in the presence of the fruit that came from the tree fertilized by it.

If you look at the difficulties that must be overcome, you will be scared and will not advance.

You must only value the good to which you are committed, preserving your inner sanctum against all forms of rebellion unfolding in ill-will toward the people involved in it.

Supported by your serene faith, you will act differently than the norm during your earthly experiences.

You know through experience that, where you used to be before, there was no crime or vice but sheer ignorance and disease in the game of unnecessary afflictions. Thus, you will identify opportunities to serve where you once only saw a reason to be disgusted and to stay away, knowing that, within the narrow band of purely intellectual observations, your appreciation of the facts results from the pretentious demands of your own way of looking at things.

If you do not get rid of mordant criticism –unproductive by nature– all your efforts will be useless in the context of Christian undertakings.

Tie your feelings to the reins of true service and, driven by love in its simplest and purest form, remember Jesus. Learn with Him to do tireless work, removing blindness from people's eyes and extracting unhappiness from people's hearts. And improve and purify yourself, for if the desires of your Spirit are not placated, you will not be ready to experience serenity under the command of complete confidence.

57
INFIRM SPIRITS

Almost all of us are infirm Spirits.
We have passions.
We are entrenched in our opinions.
We control other hearts.
We demean sentiments.
We hold grudges.

Though we have been illuminated by the Divine Clarity, we hide the sun of belief behind the cloud of doubt.

Having been touched by universal love through powerful messages, we insist on cultivating idleness, scheming, invalidating hope, and empowering selfishness in petty endeavors of personal pleasure.

Although fascinated by the High Heavens, we still dream of the earth and fight for earthly power.

In the name of fraternity, we steer consciences under the whip of hostile words, acts, and thoughts.

Almost all of us are infirm Spirits…

But if the seed refuses to die, it does not give the tree the chance to live.

The water that does not submit does not move the dynamos that benefit life.

The wheat that resists being crushed will never transform into bread.

From your disease the *death* of your form will emerge, so that the spark of light of which you are constituted may grow.

No one can accuse you for bringing the mire from yesterday and the mud from today stuck in your wounded feet.

Without the furrows that pain tore in your flesh, progress would have been impossible.

Without disease, hope would have no reason for being.

Yes, almost all of us are infirm Spirits walking toward Jesus who, as the Ambassador of True Life, left the majesty of His kingdom to come to us, and in giving Himself over for the sake of us all –evolving Spirits– He became the *bread of life* to feed us during the difficult evolutionary journey.

58
THE SPIRITIST BOOK

Bless the opportunity to sow.

Tomorrow will be time to harvest.

Value the blessing of physical life on the road to eternal life. Remember that the flesh is a short-lived opportunity, and soon you will return to the spirit world, perhaps unexpectedly.

The body is a concession from God for the Spirit to learn and act, valuing the available resources.

Death leads to accountability, an evaluation of what we have learned...

Working on behalf of the good is the saving guideline.

To take advantage of the gift of time –during the season of today's opportunities– is a duty that cannot be postponed.

Tomorrow, the strong sun of despair or the glacial cold of disenchantment might not offer the spiritual climate for you to fulfill your responsibilities, while you are still in the physical body.

Right now, the light of the proper occasion shines on your path.

Later, your health might not cooperate, your hope might be dwindling, and weariness might not give you the chance.

Currently, the Spiritist teachings awaken and invite you, in honor of the Eternal Life and the Eternal Wisdom they represent.

By telling you that the earth is an arena for honest work, they remind you that you will return to the Spiritual Homeland bearing the consequences of your actions.

Open your heart to the message of imperishable life, and apply the treasures that Spiritism gives you for the happiness of all.

Today, you head toward the blessed sowing, and suffering hearts await the valuable concession of faith.

Spread the light that illuminates your own path by helping indiscriminately.

You must give shelter to the faith that liberates and purifies you, helping those who are still not harboring it. In that sense, remember the Spiritist book. Bring it into your heart, and it will provide you with warmth and joy for your life.

An edifying teaching constitutes a blessing everywhere. A Spiritist lesson is a light along the path.

Thus, turn on that sublime light on the narrow passage through which many people walk in total darkness.

If they do not understand you, learn to forgive.

If you run into obstacles preventing you from being successful, try to understand the nature of the struggle and benefit from it.

Wherever the Spiritist teachings appear, the hands of Jesus also emerge, serving and helping.

Thus, you will discover in Spiritism that charity is the soul of life, vitalizing everything.

In that sense, bread for the stomach and clothing to cover nakedness is immediate help, while the luminous words —born in the heart of the Master and transmitted by the Spiritist book— is lasting bread and an eternal seed of light.

A Spiritist letter consoles.

A Spiritist lesson teaches.

Spiritist help enlightens.

A Spiritist book liberates and steers in the right direction.

It is for this reason that —honoring the noble and constructive book— The Spirit of Truth said, *"O Spiritist! Love one another; this is the first teaching. Educate yourselves; this is the second,"* vehemently affirming that *"Jesus Christ is the victor over evil; be victors over impiety."*[12]

Honor the Spiritist book and disseminate it with the strength of your love for the good, and you will see —as early as tomorrow— the earthly orb filled with the consoling hope provided by Spiritism, in whose core the souls will find rest for all their weariness.

---

12 *The Gospel According to Spiritism*, by Allan Kardec, Ch. VI, "The Coming of the Spirit of Truth," Item 5 (International Spiritist Council). – Tr.

59
JESUS IN THE HOME

Dedicate one of your seven evenings to the practice of The Gospel at Home, so that Jesus may spend the night at your house.

Prepare the table, set a pitcher with fresh water, gather the family, open the Gospel, read the message of faith, and pray. Jesus will come to visit.

When the home becomes a sanctuary, crime withdraws. When the family prays, Jesus stays in the home. When hearts unite through the ties of faith, equilibrium provides the blessing of consolation, and good health pours the wine of peace for everyone.

Jesus in the Home is life for the Home.

Do not wait for the world to bring you the certainty of the invariable good. Spread from your Christian home the light of the Gospel to the tormented world.

When a family prays at home –gathered under the wonders of the Gospel– the entire street receives the benefit of being in communion with the Higher Spheres.

If someone in an apartment building sends a prayer to the Heavens in communion with the family –like a lonely lamp that remains lit despite the strong winds– the entire building benefits.

Do not deviate from the guidelines of the Gospel among your next of kin. Continue to pray faithfully and to study the Master's directives with your children and loved ones. And, whenever possible, discuss the problems that afflict you in the brilliant light of the message of the Good News, examining the difficulties that trouble you under the consoling inspiration of the Christ. Do not go out that night, unless you must fulfill essential duties that cannot be postponed. Stay at home so that the Divine Guest may linger there too.

And when you turn out the light to go to sleep, pray one more time seeking communion with Him, just like He tries to do, so that, connected to you, you may have Jesus with you at home during one of your seven weekly evenings.

60
FACING DISINCARNATION

However long a physical existence may be, it is no more than a temporary season.

Due to natural wear and tear, the body of flesh is consumed, endlessly recycling itself until it is transformed into other expressions of life –in the silence of the soil– after it has been abandoned by the Spirit.

Everything that is born dies –that is the Law.

Reincarnation is a much-needed learning opportunity of brief duration.

For that reason, the body is a vehicle with which the Divinity honors Its children, affording them the opportunity to ascend to the celestial planes.

They all die in one vibrational state to be reborn in another. There is no annihilation. Life goes on!

Beyond the portal of mud and ashes, life goes on like a beautiful springtime after a dark and tormenting night.

Love those who were instrumental to your physical life or the reason for your happiness, without forcing them to stay longer amid the limitations of the physical vessel.

They miss the Great Spiritual Homeland and long to return, despite the factors that retain them along the way.

Do not torment them with your love. They will remain with you in a different state of consciousness.

They will help you with your suffering, drying your sweat and tears, and they will pray for you during your difficult hours…

Prepare them with love, informing them about life in the Greater World, and help them disentangle from the tentacles and bonds that tie them to the earth.

Remember and remind them about the sublime dawn awaiting them, explaining the triumphant nature of resurrection beyond the transitoriness of all things.

Counter your sadness with the memories of happy times together, all the good they did to you, and what they represented in your life...

While they are still by your side, benefit from their goodness and wisdom, honoring them in turn with your love and attention. Qualify yourself to receive their love through the merit of the effort that you make in the name for love.

What you do not give them now will be worth nothing tomorrow.

What you do not do now —out of negligence or carelessness— will tether you around the boulder of unproductive sorrow.

If they are old, have patience and surround them with even more love.

If they are sick, shower them with care. The vigil that you keep beside the bed of a sick person, is a deposit that you make in the Celestial Treasury.

If they are young, offer them your experience in the form of advice, assistance, discipline, and education.

If they are friends, relatives, loved ones, or acquaintances, extend your arms and embrace them with the kind of tenderness that makes life beautiful.

If they are strangers or adversaries, overcome your aversion and love them as well, helping them as much as possible to join your spiritual family.

Remember, however, that they will all leave soon...

The return is inevitable.

We begin to die the moment we are reborn in the flesh.

Their memory will make you happy, and all the good that they did to you —just as all the love you gave to them— will be the crown of light that you will wear in life.

And, lastly, remember that while being anguished by an intense longing, hidden and afraid, the disciples gathered in Jerusalem received the visit of Jesus, the unforgettable Friend, who greeted them joyously.

He returned from *death* and ensured the happiness of all –throughout millennia– with the legacy of the victory of life after disincarnation –as attested today by those who, having defeated the grave, happily return to their loved ones still in the flesh, repeating *peace be with you*, like a perpetual hymn of immortal consolation.

Made in the USA
Middletown, DE
11 August 2022

71134350R10092